Your
DAILY JOURNEY
of HOPE

Your DAILY JOURNEY *of* HOPE

Iris Fisher Smith *and* Tammy J. Maseberg

XULON PRESS

Xulon Press
2301 Lucien Way #415
Maitland, FL 32751
407.339.4217
www.xulonpress.com

© 2021 by Iris Fisher Smith and Tammy J. Maseberg

Edited by Heidi M. Thomas

All rights reserved solely by the author. The author guarantees all contents are original and do not infringe upon the legal rights of any other person or work. No part of this book may be reproduced in any form without the permission of the author. The views expressed in this book are not necessarily those of the publisher.

Due to the changing nature of the Internet, if there are any web addresses, links, or URLs included in this manuscript, these may have been altered and may no longer be accessible. The views and opinions shared in this book belong solely to the author and do not necessarily reflect those of the publisher. The publisher therefore disclaims responsibility for the views or opinions expressed within the work.

Unless otherwise indicated, Scripture quotations taken from the Holy Bible, New International Version (NIV). Copyright © 1973, 1978, 1984, 2011 by Biblica, Inc.™. Used by permission. All rights reserved.

Scripture quotations taken from the New King James Version (NKJV). Copyright © 1982 by Thomas Nelson, Inc. Used by permission. All rights reserved.

Scripture quotations taken from the Holy Bible, New Living Translation (NLT). Copyright ©1996, 2004, 2007 by Tyndale House Foundation. Used by permission of Tyndale House Publishers, Inc.

Paperback ISBN-13: 978-1-6628-3423-3
eBook ISBN-13: 978-1-6628-3424-0

How To Use This Book

"The LORD himself goes before you and will be with you; he will never leave you nor forsake you. Do not be afraid; do not be discouraged." Deuteronomy 31:8

The title we chose for this book, *Your Daily Journey of Hope*, comes from a culmination of our individual journeys. Many years ago, Iris and I began writing a newsletter together under the ministry of Joni and Friends. When someone suggested taking some of those articles and putting them together in a book, we looked at the original focus of what we had written. It was encouragement. People needed hope then, and I would venture to say they need it even more now in this present time. We have chosen Deuteronomy 31:8 as the theme verse of this book because it speaks of the promise of God that He is always with us. If He is always with us, then we are never alone and, therefore, we have hope.

Our prayer for you, the reader of this book, is that you will find hope for each day by searching and studying God's word to learn more about Him, the very One who made you and who loves you so very much. Those three concepts of hope, encouragement, and feeling like you are never alone, tie together the original newsletters, Iris's first book *Never Alone* that was published in August 2020, and Tammy's blog site. For more resources and information, see the following links:

Book, *Never Alone*: www.irisfsmith.com
Blog: "Perfect Hope for Imperfect Days" at:
www.Perfect-Hope.com

This devotional, *Your Daily Journey of Hope* at:
www.YourDailyJouneyOfHope.com

The following explains how this book is organized and some suggestions on how to get the most out of this devotional/Bible study.

Each week has an overall "theme" verse along with a short piece of writing from personal experiences and observations, by either Iris or me. Below that you will find a daily Scripture for Tuesday through the weekend days. When possible, read the verses in context – read the whole chapter and/or whole book. For example: if the verse is John 3:16, read all of John 3 or even all of the book of John. Try reading the verse in different translations. Sometimes a different translation will help you to understand the verse more clearly. After each daily verse is a "Reflect, Activate" question and/or statement for you to further explore and apply God's Word to your life. We highly encourage you to keep a journal of your thoughts, struggles, prayers, etc., throughout the year.

This book is designed to be used year after year. There are no set dates but rather the weeks are numbered 1 through 52. We have included a calendar of several years at the end of the book for your convenience.

Finally, Romans 10:9-10 says this: "If you declare with your mouth, 'Jesus is Lord,' and believe in your heart that God raised him from the dead, you will be saved. For it is with your heart that you believe and are justified, and it is with your mouth that you profess your faith and are saved."

If you don't know Jesus as your Lord and Savior or if you feel you need to renew your commitment to Him, you can pray the prayer of salvation below or something similar. Remember, this is between you and God. There is no "magic" in the words—it is simply you talking to your creator, the God who loves you so much and wants you to spend eternity with Him in heaven. He sent His Son to die and then rise again so that anyone who believes (as the verse above says) can do that. What hope we can have!

Prayer of Salvation:
"Our loving and gracious Father in heaven, I confess to you that I am a sinner and have need for You in my life. I want to spend eternity with you. If I were to die tomorrow, I want the peace of knowing where I'm going. I receive You into my heart right now. I believe I'm saved and forgiven for all my transgressions. In Jesus's name I pray, Amen."

Here are some verses pertaining the hope of salvation we can have from God the Father through Jesus Christ (all from the New International Version):

> "Jesus answered, 'I am the way and the truth and the life. No one comes to the Father except through me.'" (John 14:6)

> "He saved us, not because of righteous things we had done, but because of his mercy. He saved us through the washing of rebirth and renewal by the Holy Spirit." (Titus 3:5)

> "For it is by grace you have been saved, through faith—and this is not from yourselves, it is the gift of God—not by works, so that no one can boast." (Ephesians 2:8-9)

"For God so loved the world that he gave his one and only Son, that whoever believes in him shall not perish but have eternal life. For God did not send his Son into the world to condemn the world, but to save the world through him. Whoever believes in him is not condemned, but whoever does not believe stands condemned already because they have not believed in the name of God's one and only Son." (John 3:16-18)

"He then brought them out and asked, 'Sirs, what must I do to be saved?' They replied, 'Believe in the Lord Jesus, and you will be saved—you and your household.'" (Acts 16:30-31)

"For as in Adam all die, so in Christ all will be made alive." (1 Corinthians 15:22)

"Very rarely will anyone die for a righteous person, though for a good person someone might possibly dare to die. But God demonstrates his own love for us in this: While we were still sinners, Christ died for us. Since we have now been justified by his blood, how much more shall we be saved from God's wrath through him! For if, while we were God's enemies, we were reconciled to him through the death of his Son, how much more, having been reconciled, shall we be saved through his life!" (Romans 5:7-10)

"For even the Son of Man did not come to be served, but to serve, and to give his life as a ransom for many." (Mark 10:45)

"If we confess our sins, he is faithful and just and will forgive us our sins and purify us from all unrighteousness." (1 John 1:9)

ALL of John 15

May God bless you and keep you as you explore His word and come to know Him better and better each day! Tammy and Iris

WEEK 1

God Is With You in the Valleys

"Even though I walk through the darkest valley, I will fear no evil, for you are with me; your rod and your staff, they comfort me." (Psalms 23:4)

Throughout my life, I have watched many changes take place. I am all too aware of what the term, "valley experience" means. Think about what a physical valley looks like. It has an opening at both ends; there is a way in and a way out. As you enter the valley, you may wonder how you will get through it. The only way to reach the other side is to go through it—not around or over, but through it.

Now as I picture a valley in my mind, I think about how it relates to our own lives. If you are in a place where you have entered a valley, know this: You are already on your way through.

You need to go through this time in your life to get to the other side, and if you stop in the middle you may get stuck. But do not despair. Keep going, lean on the Lord, and let Him show you what He wants you to learn while in the valley. Look to the Lord because I believe He has a great plan for you in this. Keep pressing on until you reach the goal God has for you. He allows these valleys in our lives to help us to grow spiritually and so we can be used in other people's lives.

When you come out of valley experiences, there is always something greater and more wonderful waiting for you. Whatever you are going through, in due time God can use you in a better way than before. Then there is less of you and more of Him, and that should always be our goal. In His perfect time, He will promote you. Ask Him to change your attitude during this experience. Focus on all His promises. As you do this, He will remind you of how He has helped you before. Look up, fix your eyes on the Father, and remember all your victories in the past.

That is all; just trust Him. All He expects is loyalty, and He will take care of the rest. It is all good, and He is in control. He knows the best plan for your life. May the Lord Jesus empower you in a unique way. All His blessings to you, Iris

Tuesday
Scripture: "And the God of all grace, who called you to his eternal glory in Christ, after you have suffered a little while, will himself restore you and make you strong, firm and steadfast." (1 Peter 5:10)

Reflect, Activate: Think of a time you were going through a "valley experience." How did God bring you through it? Perhaps you are still walking in it. How are you stronger because of it?

Wednesday
Scripture: "God is not unjust; he will not forget your work and the love you have shown him as you have helped his people and continue to help them." (Hebrews 6:10)

Reflect, Activate: Think about when someone helped you during a time when you really needed it. Perhaps tell that person how grateful you are for that. Consider how God helps us sometimes by sending people to be His hands and feet. Do you know someone who needs help? Is there anything you can do?

Thursday
Scripture: "'Though the mountains be shaken and the hills be removed, yet my unfailing love for you will not be shaken nor my covenant of peace be removed,' says the Lord, who has compassion on you." (Isaiah 54:10)

Reflect, Activate: Reflect on the beauty in the world. That could be an amazing view of the ocean, a song with a beautiful melody, the taste of your favorite food, or the twinkle in a child's eye. Think about how much God loves us and how He has given us beautiful things to enjoy.

Friday
Scripture: "For I know the plans I have for you," declares the Lord, "plans to prosper you and not to harm you, plans to give you hope and a future." (Jeremiah 29:11)

Reflect, Activate: Think about how God used one of your "valley experiences" so you could later help someone going through a similar thing.

Saturday/Sunday
Scripture: "And we know that all things work together for good to those who love God, to those who are the called according to His purpose." (Romans 8:28, NKJV)

Reflect, Activate: Think about an incident in your life that seemed negative at the time. Then how later you could see God's good and a better plan unfold because of it.

Prayer for the Week: Dear God, we all know people who are struggling through a valley experience right now. I ask that you send people to help them and provide for their every need. Show me how I can encourage or help someone in a practical way for I know we, your children, are Your hands and feet. You not only know the valley they are walking through but also the one I am in right now. Show me the paths to take in this time of uncertainty and/or darkness and what You want to teach me. Fill my heart with the hope and comfort that can only come from You. In Jesus' Name, Amen.

WEEK 2
The Assurance of God's Presence

"...God has said, 'Never will I leave you; never will I forsake you.'"
(Hebrews 13:5b)

Don't you sometimes long for God to take you into His arms? To hold you and make you feel safe? I know I do. When things get tough in the world around me, my heart aches to feel the Lord's closeness. What a comfort it is to know that no matter what happens, God will never, ever leave us—ever! And He promises to never turn us away when we go to Him.

Even though we may know that God is with us, sometimes we just need a person "with skin on" to physically hold us or to encourage us during our most difficult times. Or maybe it is us who will be there for someone else who is struggling through challenging circumstances. We tend to look for people who make us feel that no matter how upside down our world gets, we will stay upright.

But people come and go in our lives. Very few will play primary roles for the duration; most will only be part of our lives for a season. It can be difficult to understand why some relationships do not last. However, the hope we have is that God's plan for us is bigger and more intricate than our minds can fathom. He knows what and who we need, and then He will bring all things together in His perfect timing.

We can be certain that God will not let us down—unlike people who may not be there for us when we need them the most—either out of choice or circumstances. We can rest assured that He is not fickle with His love for us. He is God, and what He says He means.

Psalm 34:18 says that the Lord is close to the brokenhearted. (See Friday verse below). Think about those words and let them sink deep into your heart. Then allow the Lord to take you to the place where He can bind up your broken heart and tend to your gaping wounds. No matter what you are going through or what negative voices try to invade your thinking, God loves you and is with you through it all. Be encouraged, Tammy

Tuesday
Scripture: "...those the Father has given me will come to me, and I will never reject them." (Matthew 6:37, NLT)

Reflect, Activate: Think of a time you were rejected by someone. Now, set your mind and heart on the fact that the Lord will never do that to you. If you know someone who is experiencing rejection, offer them words of encouragement and comfort.

Wednesday
Scripture: "As the rain and the snow come down from heaven, and do not return to it without watering the earth and making it bud and flourish, so that it yields seed for the sower and bread for the eater, so is My word that goes out from My mouth. It will not return to Me empty, but will accomplish what I desire and achieve the purpose for which I sent it." (Isaiah 55:10-11)

Reflect, Activate: Search the Bible for specific promises from God. Write them down and then go back and re-read as many times as you need to.

Thursday
Scripture: "God is not human, that he should lie, not a human being, that he should change his mind. Does he speak and then not act? Does he promise and not fulfill?" (Numbers 23:19)

Reflect, Activate: When did someone make a promise to you but then did not follow through with it? Forgive that person and then focus on all of God's promises. Remember—He will never go back on His promises. When have you not fulfilled a promise to someone else? Make it right! Talk to them if possible, admit your wrongdoing, and then ask for their forgiveness.

Friday
Scripture: "The Lord is close to the brokenhearted and saves those who are crushed in spirit." (Psalm 34:18)

Reflect, Activate: Do you know someone who is brokenhearted? If possible, call them or send a card or even a gift. This will lift their spirits as you act as God's hands and feet.

Saturday and Sunday
Scripture: "There is a time for everything, and a season for every activity under the heavens." (Ecclesiastes 3:1)

Reflect, Activate: There are many different seasons in each of our lives. Think back on seasons you have passed through, and then think on where you are now and how you grew through each of those seasons.

Prayer for Week: Lord, thank You for the people You have put into my life to comfort, encourage, and disciple me when I needed it. Praise You that You never leave us or forsake us!

WEEK 3

God Is With You During Times of Suffering

"Consider it pure joy, my brothers and sisters, whenever you face trials of many kinds, because you know that the testing of your faith produces perseverance." (James 1:2-3)

Suffering is a test of faith. I think of my friend, Elaine, who had cancer many years ago. She knew what it is was like to suffer. Yet, I watched her persevere. I saw her encourage others as if the word "cancer" did not intimidate her at all, and I believe it didn't. This woman loved and trusted the Lord so much. She knew no matter what, she could do all things through Christ who gave strength to her. She was willing to do whatever He asked of her because it meant lives would be touched and changed and strengthened for Him; even changed for eternity. Another friend of mine, Peggy, also suffered with cancer. During her time of trial, I saw an exuberant woman who knew beyond a shadow of a doubt that God allowed the struggle of the cancer in her life. She felt the purpose of the tribulation of her illness was to refine, purify, and strengthen her to be able to serve Him in a greater way. What a testimony!

Can we have the same attitude as these two ladies? If God's love calls you in suffering, embrace the situation with the enthusiasm for the opportunities He will provide through it. My friend, I do not know what physical or emotional challenges you may be experiencing today. But would you look to the Lord for the reasons why He may be asking you to go through this? Could the purpose be, as the Bible says, so we can be there for others?

Is it possible that our afflictions and suffering are to make us stronger and better able to serve Him? We may never know all the reasons. It is only in spending time with God by reading His Word in the Bible and praying to Him that you will begin to see His perfect plan unfold in your life. Then you can watch Him skillfully use circumstances to encourage and make a difference in someone else's life. If God can encourage one person through your trials and suffering or someone else comes to know Him, isn't it worth it? You see, God loves you so much that He has entrusted you with the suffering He has called you to, so you can be used in a greater way. I am certain God has a special plan for you. I encourage you to seek Him and ask Him to reveal the direction He would have you go to fill the destiny He has called you to.

Whether your circumstances take you to a new place to be used in your earthly ministry for Him or even if He is calling you home, God still has a hope and a future for you and for each one of us. Just look to Him and you will truly see that it is all good! May the Lord bless you mightily and for His glory! Iris

Tuesday
Scripture: "And the God of all grace, who called you to his eternal glory in Christ, after you have suffered a little while, will himself restore you and make you strong, firm and steadfast." (1 Peter 5:10)

Reflect, Activate: When did you have a time of suffering and what did you learn from God through it?

Wednesday
Scripture: "Praise be to the God and Father of our Lord Jesus Christ, the Father of compassion and the God of all comfort, who comforts us in all our troubles, so that we can comfort those in any trouble with the comfort we ourselves have received from God. For just as the sufferings of Christ flow over into our lives, so also through Christ our comfort overflows." (2 Corinthians 1:3-5)

Reflect, Activate: How have you been able to help someone who is or was going through something similar to a trial you went through in the past?

Thursday
Scripture: "'For I know the plans I have for you,' declares the LORD, 'plans to prosper you and not to harm you, plans to give you hope and a future. Then you will call upon me and come and pray to me, and I will listen to you. You will seek me and find me when you seek me with all your heart.'" (Jeremiah 29: 11-13)

Reflect, Activate: Do you know someone who is suffering? Can you encourage them that God has a plan for them, even though it is difficult to see right now?

Friday
Scripture: "I can do all things through Christ who strengtheneths me." (Philippians 4:13, NKJV)

Reflect, Activate: Is there a situation in your life right now that you need to trust in God's strength to get you through?

Saturday and Sunday
Scripture: "being confident of this, that he who began a good work in you will carry it on to completion until the day of Christ Jesus." (Philippians 1:6)

Reflect, Activate: Is there an area in your life that you feel God has begun a "good work" but the process is still going on? How have you seen that progress over time? Think about where you were and how far He has brought you.

Prayer for the Week: Dear God, thank You for all You have done in my life to help me in my times of suffering and trial. When I go through struggles, help me to not waste the experience but to learn all that You would have me learn. Show me any people around me who are experiencing pain and suffering and then lead me in how I can help and encourage them. In Jesus' name, Amen.

WEEK 4
Adapting, Adjusting, Living Well

"'Though the mountains be shaken and the hills be removed, yet my unfailing love for you will not be shaken nor my covenant of peace be removed,' says the LORD, who has compassion on you." (Isaiah 54:10)

My grandma was in her mid-90s when she died some years ago. She was still living independently in her own house. In His mercy, God called her home before she went through a lengthy illness or significant decline of her cognitive abilities. What a way to go!

Think of all the changes she saw in the world through nine decades of living: the Great Depression, World War II, the assassination of a President, man walking on the moon, etc. Color television, computers, and organ transplants all came into existence during her lifetime. On a personal level, she experienced blessings and tragedies just like anyone else. She was a widow for almost 50 years. As a single mom she watched two of her sons go off to serve in the Vietnam War. By the time she was in her 90s, most of her friends had either died or were living in nursing homes. She had to deal with many losses including a daughter, a grandson, and all but one of her siblings.

The more things change, the more things stay the same. Conflicts have been a part of the world forever. No one is immune to trials in his or her own personal life. We get so caught up in thinking the way things are now is the worst it has ever been. If we look back in history, though, we will see that people before us have experienced great difficulties and changes in the world, too. Many overcame some seemingly insurmountable obstacles.

How do we adapt and survive all that life throws at us? One thing we can be assured of is that God will stay the same and He will bring good into our lives—no matter what. Regardless of what we have to face or what happens around us, He will remain who He is, and His promises will stay intact. He will help us to not just survive but also to live well.

Loved ones pass on. Friends and family move away. Children grow up and move out on their own. I was blessed to have both my grandmas into my late 40s. But do I miss them? Yes! Do I wish things could have stayed as they were and that they were still here with us? Of course. But that is not how it works. Change is inevitable, and we have to adjust.

So, if you are going through a significant change or a rough stretch in your life right now, remember this: God stays the same. He is our Rock that will not be moved, no matter how fierce the winds blow or how drastic the ups and downs of life are. Blessings, Tammy

Tuesday
Scripture: "What has been will be again, what has been done will be done again; there is nothing new under the sun." (Ecclesiastes 1:9)

Reflect, Activate: It is true – there is nothing new. However, is there some attitude or habit you feel you need to change and bring about something new into your life? Be intentional about making that change happen and ask Jesus to help you with it.

Wednesday
Scripture: "Whatever is good and perfect comes down to us from God our Father, who created all the lights in the heavens. He never changes or casts a shifting shadow. (James 1:17)

Reflect, Activate: What gifts/blessings has God given you?

Thursday
Scripture: "Truly he is my rock and my salvation; he is my fortress, I will never be shaken." (Psalm 62:2)

Reflect, Activate: Look up the definition for "stronghold." Then think about (or write down) how the Lord fits that definition in your life.

Friday
Scripture: "Jesus Christ is the same yesterday and today and forever. (Hebrews 13:8)

Reflect, Activate: Write a list of how Jesus is the always the same: "Jesus is the same in that He always_____"

Saturday and Sunday
Scripture: "I have told you all this so that you will have peace of heart and mind. Here on earth you will have many trials and sorrows; but cheer up, for I have overcome the world." (John 6:33, NLT)

Reflect, Activate: Think of someone who is going through a time of sorrow right now. Is there something you can do to bring them some cheer? Perhaps a call or card, etc.

Prayer for Week: Lord, help me to remember that You are the unchanging Rock I can lean on no matter what life may bring. Thank You for being the steadiness I need when I feel like I'm standing on shaky ground.

WEEK 5

Why Worship Cannot Wait

> "Yet this I call to mind and therefore I have hope: Because of the LORD's great love we are not consumed, for his compassions never fail. They are new every morning; great is your faithfulness." (Lamentations 3:21-23)

True happiness is not in the absence of trials; it is in the presence of God. Through worshipping Him and being in His presence, we can find true happiness, joy, peace, contentment, and all we need. Did you ever think about the fact that God gives us what we need at the very time that we need it? If our focus is on Him and His plan for our lives, He will provide for us in every way.

Think about worship for a moment. Why should we worship God while experiencing suffering? It is for our benefit, my friend. You see, the devil wants us to get into depression and worry. He wants us to get so caught up in the cares of this life, that our focus will be on what is going wrong, and not on what God has in store for us. God has great and mighty plans for us that we cannot even imagine.

When we are in the presence of God, the enemy will flee. The best way to ward off his attacks is simple: just turn your back on him and turn to God. This is done through praise and worship, prayer, sitting quietly in His presence, and standing on God's Word. His Word is sharper than any two-edged sword. It does not mean all our problems and trials will disappear. What it does mean, however, is we will have a greater supernatural ability to go through those storms in life with God's peace and perspective.

Praise and worship God in any circumstance; this is a phrase that bears repeating over and over in our minds and even out loud. When you go into your prayer closet pray, "In my sick body, God is able. In my emotionally challenging times, God is able. During a financial loss, God is able. Whatever the trial or storm, God is able. I am going to praise Him in the partial until I have the whole." Do not doubt what God can do, and do not give up. He will see you through any circumstance! Keep praising Him and you will see the faithfulness of God. He has all the power to deliver you and me out of all hopelessness and despair.

So, why can worship not wait? Because God has great and wonderful things waiting for you. While in His presence, the devil cannot hold you in a place of despair. God promises that during worship, He will take you to a place that only He can: away from hopelessness into eternal hope. God loves you so much! May God's love and presence envelop you as you love Him unconditionally, as He does you. Bless you, my friend, Iris.

Tuesday
Scripture: "Take delight in the Lord, and he will give you the desires of your heart." (Psalms 37:4)

Reflect, Activate: Today, make a conscious decision to be "delighted" in the Lord. Think on all that He had given you and done for you and then praise Him!

Wednesday
Scripture: "Submit yourselves, then, to God. Resist the devil, and he will flee from you." (James 4:7)

Reflect, Activate: Think of a time when you had to consciously resist a temptation. How did God help you?

Thursday
Scripture: "Trust in the Lord with all your heart and lean not on your own understanding; in all your ways submit to him, and he will make your paths straight." (Proverbs 3:5-6)

Reflect, Activate: When did you do the opposite of this and went down your own path, only to discover it wasn't a good thing?

Friday
Scripture: "I can do all this through him who gives me strength." (Philippians 4:13)

Reflect, Activate: When have you felt Christ's strength in a situation that you physically felt weak? Is there someone you know who thinks they are weak, but you see as strong because of their relationship with the Lord?

Saturday/Sunday
Scripture: "For the word of God is alive and active. Sharper than any double-edged sword, it penetrates even to dividing soul and spirit, joints and marrow; it judges the thoughts and attitudes of the heart." (Hebrews 4:12)

Reflect, Activate: What does this verse mean? In your life, how has the Bible been "living, active, and sharp"?

Prayer for the Week: Dear God, I praise You for Your kindness and faithfulness towards me and those around me. Help me to keep my focus on You and to turn away from the ploys of the enemy. Thank You for the strength You give me in all situations. Show me those people who need to hear the hope that can be found only in You. In Jesus' name, Amen.

WEEK 6

Do-Overs Allowed

"Because of the LORD's great love we are not consumed, for his compassions never fail. They are new every morning; great is your faithfulness." (Lamentations 3:22-23)

"Do-over!" younger brother shouts to his older brother, the pitcher.

"Whatta ya mean? That was perfect," says older brother.

"No, it wasn't. It almost hit me in the head."

"Why'd ya swing at it then? Strike three. You're out."

"No. Do-over." Older brother gives the younger boy another chance to hit a pitch.

The above conversation makes us laugh, and if you have kids, you have probably heard it many times. Or perhaps you remember this scenario with your siblings when you were growing up. As adults we sometimes want, and need, a chance to start over or a second try at re-doing something that did not turn out so well. Everyone has regrets—bad decisions, missed opportunities, and wrong roads taken. We all have those things in the past, things we can look back on and wish we could change. Think about when a new year starts and how so many people make resolutions. There is a sense of new beginnings.

There are consequences—whether good or bad—to all decisions we make. I want to believe that the majority of choices made in my life, I have done with the very best intentions in mind. When faced with a decision, I think most of us will take the best option available based on our abilities and the information we possess at that time.

What if later on, however, we realize that it was not the best choice after all? We can take heart because there is good news! God allows "do-overs." He lets us make an about-face when we find ourselves traveling the wrong way. Like the older brother in the above conversation, God has great compassion on us. He gives us a new start every day: I love that! When I have a bad day, I know the next morning is going to be new and fresh. Phew!

God is always faithful when we come to Him and tell him we have messed up (again) and would like a second chance. Then He will help us to move on. Hopefully, the next time we come up against a similar situation, we will turn to the Lord quicker to help us avoid going down that wrong road again. Remember that when you come to Christ, you enter into a new life. You no longer have to live as the "old you" would have. He will help you see and experience all things new.

So, be encouraged as you start each new day. Have hope if you are needing a "do-over." God is in the restoration business. He will guide you and love you through the process. God's blessing to you, Tammy

Tuesday
Scripture: "My dear children, I write this to you so that you will not sin. But if anybody does sin, we have an advocate with the Father—Jesus Christ, the Righteous One. He is the atoning sacrifice for our sins, and not only for ours but also for the sins of the whole world." (1 John 2:1-2)

Reflect, Activate: Be honest with yourself and prayerfully search to see if there is some sin you need to confess to the Lord. Ask for forgiveness and then move on.

Wednesday
Scripture: "If we confess our sins, He is faithful and just to forgive us *our* sins and to cleanse us from all unrighteousness." (1 John 1:9, NKJV)

Reflect, Activate: Big, little – it doesn't matter. God is ready to forgive all sins, if we ask. Think on His cleansing power and feel anew.

Thursday
Scripture: "When someone becomes a Christian, he becomes a brand new person inside. He is not the same anymore. A new life has begun!" (2 Corinthians 5:17)

Reflect, Activate: What existed in your old life (a habit, relationship, etc.) that no longer is there since becoming a Christ follower? Is there something still there in your new life that needs to be addressed and gone?

Friday
Scripture: "Praise be to the God and Father of our Lord Jesus Christ! In his great mercy he has given us new birth into a living hope through the resurrection of Jesus Christ from the dead." (1 Peter 1:3)

Reflect, Activate: What does it mean to be "born again"? Research verses pertaining to the term and look up the definition.

Saturday and Sunday
Scripture: "But those who wait on the Lord shall renew their strength; they shall mount up with wings like eagles, they shall run and not be weary, they shall walk and not faint." (Isaiah 40:31, NKJV)

Reflect, Activate: When was there a time in your life you felt as if you were waiting on the Lord? Maybe for a healing? Or an answer to a long-time prayer request? Did you feel like God gave you strength during the "waiting period"?

Prayer for Week: Lord Jesus, thank You for Your amazing love for me and for the second chances You've given me throughout my life. Guide me down the path You have laid out for me so that I don't have to make too many U-turns.

WEEK 7

God's Amazing Faithfulness

"How gracious he will be when you cry for help! As soon as he hears, he will answer you." (Isaiah 30:19b)

My Aunt Ruthie was developmentally disabled. I always grieved over the challenges she faced in her life, including some of the trials she experienced while living in nursing homes. I could not understand why she never heard me when I tried to minister to her about Jesus. However, God reminded me many times that He does not need my help.

I grew up in a Jewish family where Jesus was not spoken of. Even so, God put a burning desire in my heart to know Him, all without anyone really saying anything to me. When I was 14, He sent some neighbors to lead me in prayer to receive Jesus as my Lord and Savior. I wondered, could He do the same for

Auntie Ruthie? Well, after you read what I share next, you can discern the answer to that for yourself!

Let me back up to a time when Auntie Ruthie's mother, my grandmother Rose, was in a nursing home. I loved and adored my Bobe (meaning grandmother in Yiddish and pronounced Bubbie). She and I, along with my mother, shared so many wonderful times together. She taught me everything I love today, especially cooking. When I knew it would not be long before she passed away, I vigorously set out to speak to her about Jesus. I tried everything. Since she was hard of hearing and there was a language barrier because of her Russian roots, she was never able to hear me. I remember one time back in the early 1980s when my friend, Chris, and I went to see her in the Orthodox Jewish nursing home where she lived. Mentioning Jesus there was like yelling, "Nuclear war!"

We were sitting in the foyer amongst other elderly Jewish people and their families. I felt led to say to Bobe, "I know who the Jewish Messiah is." She, of course being hard of hearing, replied, "What?!" So, I repeated myself, only a bit louder this time: "Bobe, I know who the Jewish Messiah is." Again, her reply was, "What?!" I was getting a bit uncomfortable, as I kept repeating this louder and louder. Finally, she said, "What? Where's the fire?" I was beginning to draw attention to our conversation. I finally yelled, "Bobe, I know who the Jewish Messiah is! It's Jesus!" The whole room, of course, went strangely quiet. I think even some of the deaf people heard me, but not my Bobe. Looking very puzzled because she didn't see a fire anywhere, she called me a "meshugine" (pronounced meshugana). In Yiddish, this means, "You're nuts!" As we said our goodbyes and left, I questioned the Lord, "Why, Lord, would you not allow Bobe to hear me?"

Later, I had another idea. I knew of a Jewish/Messianic interpreter who could go to her. Surely, Bobe would hear it from her. Well, the very day the interpreter was to see my grandmother to tell her about Jesus, my Bobe passed away from a stroke. I could not understand why God allowed this. Had He forgotten about the woman who was so dear to me? Well about one month later, I got my answer. A woman from my church who did not know me that well talked to me after the service. "Iris," she said, "I feel led to tell you that God didn't forget your Bobe. You see, He has heard your cries for your grandmother. However, because of all that she went through in her life, she would not have heard it from any man. She would have rejected hearing about Jesus from you, because she would have thought you had betrayed her. To her, Christians, or anyone else who was not Jewish, were the enemies. Remember that she lived through the Russian/Bolshevik revolution and saw her family destroyed because of Jewish persecution. She also had to flee alone to America from those whom she thought were Christians. Then she saw many friends and much of their lives destroyed by Hitler. So, God took her at a time when He knew she would receive it from Him and Him alone. He has heard your prayers! Today, your Bobe is with Him." My heart rejoiced in the blessing I had received!

So, years later my Auntie Ruthie was in the same situation. Did I need to rush around and try to get her saved? No. As with my grandmother, I could not do something that was God's job. I knew He was fully capable of hearing my cries for Auntie Ruthie's salvation as well. My responsibility was not for her salvation but to intercede for her in prayer. The Holy Spirit would speak to her heart in the way she needed, and He would draw her to Himself. It is He who draws our unsaved loved ones to the Lord, not us. If God chooses to send someone to help, great! If not, God has a plan, and He knew what was needed to get Auntie Ruthie saved, just as with my Bobe.

Whose salvation are you praying for today? Trust God and watch miracles take place. Have you received Jesus into your heart as your Lord and Savior? If not, find a prayer for salvation on within the "How to Use This Devotional" section at beginning of this book. Bless you, my friend, Iris

Tuesday
Scripture: "This is the confidence we have in approaching God: that if we ask anything according to his will, he hears us." (1 John 5:14)

Reflect, Activate: Are you sometimes hesitant to go to God in prayer, thinking your request is too trivial or that He will not hear you for some reason? Read the above verse again; allow it to take root in your heart.

Wednesday
Scripture: "And the God of all grace, who called you to his eternal glory in Christ, after you have suffered a little while, will himself restore you and make you strong, firm and steadfast." (1 Peter 5:10)

Reflect, Activate: Reflect on a time you came out of a place of suffering and how God did just as He promises in the above verse. Is there someone you can encourage to hang in there because God will see them through?

Thursday
Scripture: "…Was my arm too short to deliver you? Do I lack the strength to rescue you?" (Isaiah 50:2b)

Reflect, Activate: Being completely honest, what trial in your life right now do you think is too difficult for God to resolve? Ask Him to boost your faith and change your thinking because of what God says in the above verse.

Friday
Scripture: "Jesus looked at them and said, 'With man this is impossible, but with God all things are possible.'" (Matthew 6:19)

Reflect, Activate: What in your life today seems impossible? Trust God to make it into a possible situation.

Saturday and Sunday
Scripture: "Know therefore that the LORD your God is God; he is the faithful God, keeping his covenant of love to a thousand generations of those who love him and keep his commandments." (Deuteronomy 7:9)

Reflect, Activate: Focus on how much God loves you (He truly does) and that He never goes back on His promises.

Prayer for the Week: Lord thank You for Your saving grace in my life. Right now, I lift up those people I know, and even those I don't know, who need to come to know You for their salvation. Help me to be aware of opportunities to talk to people about You and to always realize it is You who will draw them to Yourself. In Jesus' Name, Amen.

WEEK 8

Protection Against Sinking

> "Lord, if it's you," Peter replied, "tell me to come to you on the water." Come," he said. Then Peter got down out of the boat, walked on the water and came toward Jesus. But when he saw the wind, he was afraid and, beginning to sink, cried out, "Lord, save me!" (Matthew 14: 28-30)

We read this passage and wonder how Peter could have been full of trust and walking on the water one minute and then, in an instant, sinking beneath the surface. It is obvious to us, 2,000 years later, that he stayed on top of the waves as long as he kept his eyes on Jesus. Peter, Peter—how could you be so faithless, so flaky?

Oh, I think I am very much like Peter. The storms of life come along (illness, financial struggles, etc.), and I wonder why I feel like I am sinking deep into the dark, dangerous water of life. If I step back and get still before God—I will have to admit that I took my eyes off the Lord. Why is it so easy to look at the turmoil nearby instead of focusing on the One who can save us from seemingly overpowering circumstances?

My humanness is so frustrating sometimes! It is not that God turns away from me—it is that I turn away from Him and try to do things on my own. The Lord has brought me through so many difficult times. So, why do I still take my eyes off Him when the noise in life is surrounding and overwhelming me? Instead, my concentration drifts to the things of the world—good and bad—and I forget about my Savior. Like Peter, I soon find myself sinking and calling out to the Lord for deliverance and restoration. But there is good news! Even though Peter's distress was because of his lack of faith at that moment, Jesus rescued him. The Bible says Jesus rescued Peter immediately (see Matthew 14:31 below).

Let that sink in. Peter did not have to beg his Savior to help him. Jesus did not insist that Peter first build up that shaky faith before He reached out and saved him from drowning. No, He rescued the frightened disciple right then before the waves could completely overtake him. However, Jesus did want Peter and the others to learn from what happened. Hopefully, the next time one of them met a challenge, they were able to keep their eyes on Jesus.

So, take heart—God is with you. Focus on Him and His promises. He will not let you sink, and He will bring you through whatever you are facing right now. Call on Him. Let Him be your Savior. His love and blessing, Tammy

Tuesday
Scripture: "Immediately Jesus reached out his hand and caught him. 'You of little faith,' he said, 'why did you doubt?' And when they climbed into the boat, the wind died down. Then those who were in the boat worshiped him, saying, 'Truly you are the Son of God.'" (Matthew 14:31-33)

Reflect, Activate: Is there something going on that has caused you to take your eyes off Jesus and has made you feel as if you are sinking into the deep? Look up synonyms for the word, "immediately." Know that Jesus is there to pull you out of the water and save you right now.

Wednesday
Scripture: "But I pray to you, Lord, in the time of your favor; in your great love, O God, answer me with your sure salvation. Rescue me from the mire, do not let me sink; deliver me from those who hate me, from the deep waters." (Psalm 69:13-14)

Reflect, Activate: What lesson have you had that you can pinpoint as a turning point in your faith? How did you apply it to incidents after?

Thursday
Scripture: "I sought the Lord, and He heard me, and delivered me from all my fears." (Psalm 34:4, NKJV)

Reflect, Activate: Think about a time you were full of fear or dread and how the Lord pulled you out of that fear.

Friday
Scripture: "He has delivered us from such a deadly peril, and he will deliver us again. On him we have set our hope that he will continue to deliver us." (2 Corinthians 1:10)

Reflect, Activate: Do you know someone who has been delivered from a life-threatening situation? How did that boost your faith?

Saturday and Sunday
Scripture: "Then they cried out to the Lord in their trouble, and He saved them out of their distresses." (Psalm 107:19, NKJV)

Reflect, Activate: Thank Him that He saves us from our distresses! Write down verses pertaining to God's promises of helping us in our troubles.

Prayer for Week: Lord, thank You that You hear us when we pray and for rescuing me in those times when I cried out to You in distress.

WEEK 9

The Power of Prayer

"When you pass through the waters, I will be with you; and when you pass through the rivers, they will not sweep over you. When you walk through the fire, you will not be burned; the flames will not set you ablaze." (Isaiah 43:2)

Our son, Paul, graduated from Embry-Riddle Aeronautical University a few years ago. For his graduation present, we, along with my father, sent Paul on a cruise with his fraternity. We prepared, as usual, with prayer by asking God to keep our son safe and that he would receive at least one divine appointment along the way. We also wanted him to experience a time of refreshment and rest from all his studies.

The ship set sail on a Sunday in March. Paul and his fraternity brothers (25 in all) began their voyage with various stops in the Cayman Islands; Cozumel, Mexico; Montego Bay, Jamaica; and the Bahamas. While Paul was enjoying his vacation, I began to feel an uneasiness about his trip. By Tuesday, I was really feeling like something was wrong. The unsettling in my spirit was still there on Wednesday evening. By 4 a.m. Thursday morning, I was up and feeling an urgent need to intercede on Paul's behalf. Later that morning, I called my father and stepmother. They had also felt the same uneasiness and said they had been awake most of the night praying, too. My friend Chris called at 9:30 saying she had been led to pray also. We kept praying, not aware of that was taking place in the natural.

At 9:45 that morning my friend, Carolyn, came over to help me clean. Somehow, we got distracted with things and did not realize Paul had called. He left a message that went something like this: "Mom, I called to tell you that there's been a fire on the ship. We're okay but watch the news, and I'll try to call you later."

My heart sank because I had missed his call. So, we turned on CNN and saw the news bulletin about the fire. My stomach did flip-flops as we watched the towering inferno of flames and smoke billow from the ship. I immediately called my father and stepmother and Joni and Friends Ministry for prayer. Carolyn also prayed and encouraged me. The remainder of the day was spent watching the news and waiting to hear how everything was going.

Around 5 p.m., Paul called me from Montego Bay, Jamaica, to tell me the good news that he and all of his fraternity buddies were okay. He related to me what happened. Two of Paul's friends were up on deck at 4 a.m. when the fire broke out. They saw the blaze and began waking people up. The fire was started by a cigarette in one of the cabins, spreading very quickly to 150 cabins. Paul and his friends tried to open a door and smoke and fire were on the other side. Although the fire was all around them, Paul's cabin was undamaged and untouched. By God's grace they made it to safety. There were a lot of injuries, mostly due to smoke inhalation. However, there was only one death, a 75-year-old man who had a heart attack from all the excitement. Was it a coincidence that 150 rooms were damaged by smoke and fire and only one death occurred? I don't think so. Was it a coincidence that I was awakened at 4 a.m., along with my father, to pray? Again, I don't think so.

You see, I believe the Lord prompted me and the others, too, to pray on behalf of what was happening on that ship and to prevent an even greater disaster. I know things could have turned out much worse. In this life, we will never completely understand the power of prayer.

The magnitude of answered prayer makes me grateful that we can turn to our Father, day or night. Peace comes in, just as it did that day when we knew our son was in very capable hands even though there was nothing we could do in the natural realm. At a time when we were helpless to do anything in a situation, God was in control.

God cares when we call out to Him. Whatever you are trusting Him for, know this: we serve a God who never slumbers or turns a deaf ear to our needs. Bless you, my friend, Iris

Tuesday
Scripture: "Trust in the LORD with all your heart and lean not on your own understanding; in all your ways submit to him, and he will make your paths straight." (Proverbs 3:5-6)

Reflect, Activate: Is there a situation you need to turn over completely to God? Ask Him to help you do that and then trust that He will show the right path to take.

Wednesday
Scripture: "He will not let your foot slip—he who watches over you will not slumber; indeed, He who watches over Israel will neither slumber nor sleep. The Lord watches over you—the Lord is your shade at your right hand; the sun will not harm you by day, nor the moon by night. The Lord will keep you from all harm—he will watch over your life; the Lord will watch over your coming and going both now and forevermore." (Psalm 121:3-8)

Reflect, Activate: Remember that the Lord is available to approach 24 hours a day, 7 days a week. Ask Him to help you rest in the fact that He is always with you, protecting and watching over you.

Thursday
Scripture: "For now we see only a reflection as in a mirror; then we shall see face to face. Now I know in part; then I shall know fully, even as I am fully known." (1 Corinthians 13:12)

Reflect, Activate: Think about a time when you were awakened in the night (or felt an urge in the daytime) to pray. Maybe you didn't even know what or who you were supposed to pray for. Did you find out later that there was something serious going on, just like when Iris' son was involved in the fire on the ship?

Friday
Scripture: "Cast all your anxiety on him because he cares for you." (1 Peter 5:7)

Reflect, Activate: Practice this! When an anxious thought comes into your mind, consciously turn it over to Jesus. Continue doing this tomorrow and beyond. Soon it will become a habit.

Saturday and Sunday
Scripture: "Be anxious for nothing, but in everything by prayer and supplication, with thanksgiving, let your requests be made known to God; and the peace of God, which surpasses all understanding, will guard your hearts and minds through Christ Jesus." (Philippian 4:6-7, NKJV)

Reflect, Activate: Everyone has times when they feel afraid or alone. What are you anxious about today? Read the above verse over and over and ask God to help you give whatever is making you anxious to Him.

Prayer for the Week: Lord Jesus, when I feel anxious, help me to give it over to You in prayer. Thank You for the peace You bring to my heart when I truly stop carrying those burdens that only You are meant to shoulder. Show me people in my life whom I can encourage each day with Your love. In Jesus' name, Amen.

WEEK 10

Dealing With the Residue

> "He will cover you with his feathers, and under his wings you will find refuge; His faithfulness will be your shield and rampart. You will not fear the terror of night, nor the arrow that flies by day. For he will command his angels concerning you to guard you in all your ways; they will lift you up in their hands, so that you will not strike your foot against a stone." (Psalm 91: 4-5, 11-12)

Two of my boys and I were sitting at a light, the third car back, when a garbage truck took the corner too fast. It tipped up on two wheels and nearly fell over on us. I could not react to move the car out of the way. Had the driver not been able to right the truck and be on his way, we would have been crushed.

Did we survive? Yes. Did God protect us and the others? Yes—absolutely. The initial event lasted how long? Five seconds, tops. Then why did my insides feel all wiggly for the rest of the day? It is not because I questioned whether or not we were okay. I knew we were. Or if God had been the One to protect us. I knew I had experienced a miracle firsthand and, yet, the after affect—the residue—of what happened lingered for hours. Even when I was not thinking about the incident, my body remembered and would not stop shaking.

As I contemplate this incident now and then, I realize God does not just help us through the initial "stab-in-the-heart" situations of life. He will also be with us through all the aftermath which can sometimes be the most challenging time of all. Crises are inevitable. No one is immune to bad things and challenges happening. They can seem to present themselves at the most inopportune times.

Think about the woman whose husband of 40 years died and left her a widow. When the funeral is over and everyone goes home, she must face a different way of living. We like to label this as a "new normal." To her, nothing will be the same ever again. What about six months down the road when the phone calls and visits from friends and family stop coming so frequently? Life goes on per usual for everyone else while hers remains shattered. We know the Lord will provide her with the courage she needs to live in her new circumstances. But that does not mean it will be easy. What a comfort and joy to know He will never leave us to deal with anything alone. I am convinced that Jesus has us firmly in His loving arms in the aftermath of life's changes and traumatic situations—those things that send us reeling. He helps us deal with the everyday "stuff" as we pick up the pieces and try get back to some kind of normalcy.

How do I know this is true? Because He has done it for me and others around me over and over. I have watched people deal with incredible tragedies and losses and come out on the other side with a level of faith and perseverance they never knew existed. Nothing that comes our way can separate us from Jesus or His help. Do not let the world tell you something different.

So, if you find yourself struggling in any way, take heart. God will stay by your side and see you through by building your faith and filling you with His peace. May you feel His presence today, Tammy.

Tuesday

Scripture: "Now may the Lord of peace himself give you peace at all times and in every way. The Lord be with all of you." (2 Thessalonians 3:16)

Reflect, Activate: The possibility of peace in some circumstances may seem unlikely. Yet, the promise in the above verse says otherwise. Think about situations of great anxiety (such as a bad storm, loss of a loved one). When has Jesus provided unexplainable peace for you during a very difficult time?

Wednesday

Scripture: "When the members of the Sanhedrin heard this, they were furious and gnashed their teeth at him. But Stephen, full of the Holy Spirit, looked up to heaven and saw the glory of God, and Jesus standing at the right hand of God." (Acts 7:54-55)

Reflect, Activate: Look up other accounts in the Bible when people faced horrible things and yet had peace. How is it possible?

Thursday

Scripture: "The LORD himself goes before you and will be with you; he will never leave you nor forsake you. Do not be afraid; do not be discouraged." (Deuteronomy 31:8)

Reflect, Activate: What do you think it means that He goes before us? How does this comfort you?

Friday
Scripture: "When I said, 'My foot is slipping,' your unfailing love, LORD, supported me. When anxiety was great within me, your consolation brought me joy." (Psalm 94:18-19)

Reflect, Activate: Look up and write a list of Scriptures that comfort you when your heart is anxious.

Saturday and Sunday
Scripture: "Can anything ever separate us from Christ's love? Does it mean he no longer loves us if we have trouble or calamity, or are persecuted, or hungry, or destitute, or in danger, or threatened with death? No, despite all these things, overwhelming victory is ours through Christ, who loved us. And I am convinced that nothing can ever separate us from God's love. Neither death nor life, neither angels nor demons, neither our fears for today nor our worries about tomorrow—not even the powers of hell can separate us from God's love. No power in the sky above or in the earth below—indeed, nothing in all creation will ever be able to separate us from the love of God that is revealed in Christ Jesus our Lord." (Romans 8:35, 37-39, NLT)

Reflect, Activate: Contemplate how much God loves you! So many people need to know this. If there is someone you can think of who needs to hear that simple concept, tell them today—in a phone call or card or message somehow.

Prayer for Week: Thank You for Your divine protection over us, sometimes even when we do not realize we need protecting.

WEEK 11

Growing Up in God (All Greatness Is Born Out of Adversity)

"...until we all reach unity in the faith and in the knowledge of the Son of God and become mature, attaining to the whole measure of the fullness of Christ." Then we will no longer be infants, tossed back and forth by the waves, and blown here and there by every wind of teaching and by the cunning and craftiness of people in their deceitful scheming. Instead, speaking the truth in love, we will grow to become in every respect the mature body of him who is the head, that is, Christ. (Ephesians 4:13-15)

Growing Up in God (All Greatness Is Born Out of Adversity)

Growing up in God: What does that mean and why is it necessary? Why does God allow us to go through difficulties to help us grow up? My friends, all greatness is born out of adversity! Let me elaborate. You see, God brings the promise of His provision through His Word. We lean on those promises, knowing that what we ask for is certain. But sometimes problems do arise. Right behind those, though, is His provision. However, there are tests in between the problem and the provision. These trials are there to help us to grow up in Him. Growing up in God happens when we are put to the test and refined in the fiery furnace of affliction and adversity (see Daniel, chapter 3). During these times we are pruned and watered for greatness in God's kingdom. We know that greatness in God's eyes is different from the "greatness" that the world sees.

When we see God's hand of provision over and over again while we are the middle of a problem, we will have less and less fear. He will build up our faith and trust in Him each time we go through a valley of adversity. We become stronger, tougher, more dependent on Him and better able to serve Him. We will have greater compassion for others and a boldness for life.

In this present age, I think people have a misconception of what life should be like. We have been taught by society that life is all about reprieve with maybe a few trials in between. Actually, life is full of challenges and trials with periods of rest. You see, our temporary hardships work for good. God disciplines those whom He loves. If we allow it, God can and will use our adversities and challenges to lead us into what He has called us to do. Trials come in many forms, such as sickness, disabilities, problems at work, relationships issues, etc. We can learn to handle things differently in life and how we treat others through the difficulties we encounter. In other words, trials can help us grow up and become more mature in Christ.

Jesus always dealt with people and situations using kindness and love, and that is what He wants us to do. Our human nature without Him is drawn to do the opposite. We are born self-centered. It is through Christ that we learn to do it His way, yielding to Him and truly growing up. Follow His example, continue to grow, and He will use you in ways beyond what you could have dreamed of or done on your own.

I want to share one example. Picture how an athlete developed his ability in a sport. He was not suddenly able to run a 26-mile marathon or score points in a basketball game. He went through a lot discipline, perseverance, and even pain during training to strengthen himself and develop the necessary skills in his sport. This is not easy; it is actually quite difficult. To give his body strength and to become a first-class athlete, he had to sweat and sacrifice day after day until he was ready. God wants us to train to become spiritual athletes. It takes regular mega doses of His Word and discipline to accomplish this. Remember—it is all good! God has His hand in everything if you let Him. He will not let you go. He knows beyond our imaginations what is best for us and what we need.

So, my friends, grow up with grace, and run the race with great perseverance until you reach the finish line. At that time, you will go home to our heavenly Father where you will get your reward for the race you have run on this earth through many adversities. You will hear Him say, "Well done, my good and faithful servant." It will be well worth it! Have you considered where you will be after you have finished your race here on earth? You can receive Jesus into your heart to be the Lord and Savior of your life. If you want assurance of your eternity in heaven, pray the prayer of salvation on page 3 of this book. Be blessed, Iris.

Tuesday
Scripture: "And my God will meet all your needs according to the riches of his glory in Christ Jesus." (Philippians 4:19)

Reflect, Activate: Do you believe God supplies our needs only in those things we can see such as food, shelter, etc.? Or do you think He also supplies those needs that are intangible such as emotional, spiritual, etc.?

Wednesday
Scripture: "That is why, for Christ's sake, I delight in weaknesses, in insults, in hardships, in persecutions, in difficulties. For when I am weak, then I am strong." (2 Corinthians 12:10)

Reflect, Activate: Think back on a time when you did not know how a particular need in your life was going to be fulfilled. It may have looked impossible in the natural. How did God meet that need? Was it through a person or in some other way? Do you know someone in need who you can help in a practical way?

Thursday
Scripture: "I consider that our present sufferings are not worth comparing with the glory that will be revealed in us." (Romans 8:18)

Reflect, Activate: If you are suffering today, know that what God says in the verse above is true. Is there someone you know who is struggling, whether physically or emotionally, whom you can encourage with a phone call or card, etc.?

Friday
Scripture: "Therefore, since we are surrounded by such a great cloud of witnesses, let us throw off everything that hinders and the sin that so easily entangles. And let us run with perseverance the race marked out for us," (Hebrews 12:1)

Reflect, Activate: Run hard! Ask God to help you have endurance during your present difficulty and that people around you will see where your hope and strength comes from.

Saturday and Sunday
Scripture: "Do not conform to the pattern of this world, but be transformed by the renewing of your mind. Then you will be able to test and approve what God's will is—his good, pleasing and perfect will." (Romans 12:2)

Reflect, Activate: If you are struggling with a temptation to "do as the world is doing" – ask God to renew your mind and follow His leading, not the world's.

Prayer for the Week: Lord, help me to train for the race we are all in while on this earth. Give me strength to face any difficulties that arise each day and courage to turn away from the temptation to handle them in a worldly fashion. When I suffer, give me the endurance I need to make it through. Help me to keep a heavenly perspective that what is to come will be glorious and worth all the trouble of this life. In Jesus' Name, Amen.

WEEK 12

Black Eyes and Bullies

"In God I trust and am not afraid. What can man do to me?" (Psalm 56:11)

Most everyone recognizes the familiar whistle and opening melody from *The Andy Griffith Show*. We are transported back in time and reminded of a less complicated day gone by. Andy and Opie are strolling toward their favorite fishing hole to spend time together as father and son. Aunt Bee is at home making pot roast and apple pie. The town men are sitting outside Floyd's Barber Shop drinking bottles of soda pop and shooting the breeze. Somewhat idealistic? Yes. But I feel lessons taught on the show can still be relevant for today.

One episode features Opie being intimidated by a bigger boy. He bullies Opie into paying him a nickel each day to be granted passage down a street he has claimed as his territory. Reluctantly, Opie complies, because if he doesn't, he has promised to give him a knuckle sandwich and to pulverize him. Barney becomes suspicious, so he follows Opie one day and sees the confrontation between the two boys. Both he and Andy are heartbroken that Opie is not only afraid of his tormentor but also feels as if he cannot tell anyone of his fear.

We all have "bullies" we encounter now and then. The adult version of what Opie faced can still be manifested in the form of physical, emotional, sexual, or mental abuse. Physical abuse shows and is cruel, but the other types can be just as sinister. A child who constantly hears they are worthless will eventually believe what they have been told. Anxiety, depression, and other physical manifestations surface and cause great suffering. Illnesses, disappointments, or other losses can also be great oppressors. All these issues can prevent us from moving forward in our lives. The debilitating fear we feel can keep us in bondage, both emotionally and physically, as we struggle to get beyond the troubles plaguing us.

Opie eventually stands up to the boy. In the process of defending himself, though, he is the recipient of a black eye which he proudly shows off to his pa and Barney.

Just as Andy and Barney were sad to see Opie so frightened, I think God grieves when He sees His children full of anxiety. He does not want us to be afraid. This is clear, because He tells us over and over in the Bible to not fear but to trust in Him. God, as our heavenly Father, wants to surround us with His loving arms to comfort us during, and after, facing and standing up to the "bullies" in our lives. He is aware of what we go through and sees the scars left behind—our black eyes, so to speak.

Trust Him with your life, your whole life, even the stuff you do not want anyone else to know—those hidden scars and disfigurements. He is able and willing to carry any burden you bring to Him. He will give you all the tools you need to deal with the fear and anxiety brought on by any incident in your life. He loves you so much! Be Blessed, Tammy.

You can see the episode on www.youtube.com, search for "Opie and the Bully."

Tuesday
Scripture: "Be strong and courageous. Do not be afraid or terrified because of them, for the Lord your God goes with you; he will never leave you nor forsake you." (Deuteronomy 31:6)

Reflect, Activate: What is the bully in your life? It doesn't have to be a person. Ask God in prayer to help you face "it" and overcome your fear of it.

Wednesday
Scripture: "Surely he took up our pain and bore our suffering, yet we considered him punished by God, stricken by him, and afflicted. But he was pierced for our transgressions, he was crushed for our iniquities; the punishment that brought us peace was on him, and by his wounds we are healed." (Isaiah 53:4-5)

Reflect, Activate: Find the account in the New Testament of Jesus's suffering and death. Think about how much He loved you—and each one of us—to go through that.

Thursday
Scripture: "Do not be afraid of them, for I am with you and will rescue you," declares the LORD." (Jeremiah 1:8)

Reflect, Activate: There are many accounts in the Bible of God delivering His people from the hands of enemies. When has He done that for you? Remember—the enemy does not have to be a person. It can be a physical illness or something like depression. Perhaps it is a co-worker or boss who constantly tears you down. Then think on how God has helped you through those situations. Or perhaps you need to pray about a current one.

Friday
Scripture: "He himself bore our sins in his body on the cross, so that we might die to sins and live for righteousness; by his wounds you have been healed." (1 Peter 2:24)

Reflect, Activate: If you are struggling with a sin, go to Jesus in prayer. Ask for His forgiveness, which He is ready to give, and then remember how you have been healed through His death and resurrection.

Saturday and Sunday
Scripture: "But when they saw him walking on the lake, they thought he was a ghost. They cried out, because they all saw him and were terrified. Immediately he spoke to them and said, 'Take courage! It is I. Don't be afraid.' Then he climbed into the boat with them, and the wind died down. They were completely amazed," (Mark 6:49-51)

Reflect, Activate: How comforting to know Jesus is always with us! He is telling us to not be afraid. So, today meditate on His presence and His ability to take our fear away.

Prayer for Week: Lord, even though we will experience trouble in this world, I know You will always be by my side to help me not to be afraid. There is nothing I can face that You will not give me the courage to endure and overcome.

WEEK 13

What Is Happening and What Can We Expect?

"For in the day of trouble he will keep me safe in his dwelling; he will hide me in the shelter of His sacred tent and set me high upon a rock." (Psalm 27:5)

We are living in a day and age when things (circumstances) in our world have become so uncertain. Christians and non-Christians alike are asking questions as Bible prophecy unfolds. First, people want to know what is going to happen next in this world. Second, they are concerned about what they will go through in the future. Well, my answer to both of those questions is this: no matter what we go through or what goes on around us, we don't have to fear. God's grace will always be with us.

It is true that we are living in a dangerous world today. Radical extremists want to cause harm. Earthquakes, floods, and other natural disasters have ravaged multiple areas around the globe. People of all backgrounds have lost jobs, and many are struggling financially. But God has appointed us—you and me—to live right now during these times. It is not a mistake! Know this: God has a specific plan for you. He has a job for you to do, and you will not have to do it alone. He will send His Holy Spirit for comfort, and there will be all the peace you need during whatever you face as an individual and as a people.

I love to recall the story in the Bible of Stephen being stoned to death (see Acts 7). I used to think it must have been so painful for him, but the Bible tells us a different truth. At the end of the chapter, it says that Stephen prayed and fell asleep! This is a key point, because I believe it means Stephen never felt the pain as he was being stoned. He was so caught up in God's Spirit that he was only aware of his Lord's presence. Stephen's eyes were focused on where he was going, not where he was and what was happening to him at that point. So, I think God's grace allowed him to simply fall asleep.

My friends, whatever God calls you to experience, you will be able to face. If you are going through something for Him, I believe you, too, can be at rest, because His grace is sufficient and because He can do anything. This is true even while being tried and challenged with whatever He allows in your life for His name's sake.

So, as the world gets a little more disturbing, remember that you do not need to be afraid. God gives us the assurance He will never leave us. He offered that same promise to Joshua in the Old Testament (See Joshua 1). Moses had died, and God appointed Joshua to lead the Israelites into the Promised Land. Throughout the chapter, God gives comforting words to Joshua. He assures him that He will be right by his side. He encourages Joshua to not be afraid and that Israel will be victorious. God's plan had not changed just because of all the hardship and failure the people had brought on to themselves. The land was given to the Israelites and Joshua was to move forward in that plan with God's help. What more assurance did Joshua need? So, today we can also lean on His promise and pray for our country.

Be blessed, my friend, there is nothing to fear. God is very much in control. Encouraged by His Spirit and His hand, Iris

Tuesday
Scriptures: "The Jewish leaders were infuriated by Stephen's accusation, and they shook their fists at him in rage. But Stephen, full of the Holy Spirit, gazed steadily into heaven and saw the glory of God, and he saw Jesus standing in the place of honor at God's right hand. And he told them, 'Look, I see the heavens opened and the Son of Man standing in the place of honor at God's right hand!' Then they put their hands over their ears and began shouting. They rushed at him and dragged him out of the city and began to stone him. His accusers took off their coats and laid them at the feet of a young man named Saul." (Acts 7:54-58, NLT)

Reflect, Activate: If you have ever been accused of something you did not do, you know how difficult it can be to look at the bright side of such a situation. Yet, Stephen did by having that "eternal perspective." Is there someone you need to forgive for such a situation? Look to the Lord and recall His provision of forgiveness for you and then ask Him to help you forgive the person you need to. This is not an easy thing but remember that God will give you the grace to do it.

Wednesday
Scripture: "But he said to me, 'My grace is sufficient for you, for my power is made perfect in weakness.' Therefore, I will boast all the more gladly about my weaknesses, so that Christ's power may rest on me." (2 Corinthians 12:9)

Reflect, Activate: Reflect on God's amazing grace in your life. If you feel weak in some area, give that over to Him and watch His power do great things.

Thursday
Scripture: "Let your conduct be without covetousness; be content with such things as you have. For He Himself has said, 'I will never leave you nor forsake you' So we may boldly say:

'The LORD is my helper; I will not fear. What can man do to me?'" (Hebrews 13:5-6, NKJV)

Reflect, Activate: Look up the meaning of "covetousness." If you covet something, how could that cause you to be fearful? Is there something you covet that, perhaps, you need to pray to God about?

Friday
Scripture: "No one will be able to stand against you all the days of your life. As I was with Moses, so I will be with you; I will never leave you nor forsake you. Be strong and courageous,

because you will lead these people to inherit the land I swore to their ancestors to give them. Be strong and very courageous. Be careful to obey all the law my servant Moses gave you; do not turn from it to the right or to the left, that you may be successful wherever you go. Have I not commanded you? Be strong and courageous. Do not be afraid; do not be discouraged, for the LORD your God will be with you wherever you go." (Joshua 1:5-7, 9)

Reflect, Activate: God's plan does not change! Is there something He has been urging you to do that you need great courage in doing? Remember His promise in the above verse. God is there to help you and give you the courage and strength you need.

Saturday and Sunday
Scripture: "The LORD is good, a refuge in times of trouble. He cares for those who trust in him" (Nahum 1:7)

Reflect, Activate: Go to Him and find refuge from whatever trouble you are in today. Can you encourage someone who you know is in trying circumstances? Even a simple call or message can lift up a person.

Prayer for the Week: Lord Jesus, You know the troubles I am facing right now. I feel weak but I know that is when You are strong in my life. Give me the courage and determination to meet this situation and learn what it is you want to learn from it. Thank You that I can rest in Your promises. In Jesus Name, Amen

WEEK 14

The One Who Knows Us Best

"You have searched me, LORD, and you know me. You know when I sit and when I rise; You perceive my thoughts from afar. You discern my going out and my lying down; You are familiar with all my ways. Before a word is on my tongue You, LORD, know it completely." (Psalm 139:1-4)

Sunday morning church. A few, a hundred, or maybe even thousands of people sitting together in one room—each with a different story to tell and each with a different path traveled. A man sits alone in the back row because he does not want anyone to see the tears trickling down his face. A woman sings along with the worship songs, her face luminous with joy. What has brought the man to be downtrodden? What has the woman navigated through to be able to sing with such exultation?

It occurred to me, while sitting in church one week, that no one really knows everything that has happened in my life to bring me to the place where I am. In the same way—I do not know the whole story of that person sitting next to me. There is an old song that tells us how there is no one who knows the troubles each of have seen. It is so easy to look on the outside of a person's life and assume so many things—good or bad. We can become judgmental of why people do what they do without having all the facts. Every journey is different. Think about it—no two lives can be compared equally. There are just too many variables with backgrounds, personalities, childhood influences, experiences, etc. During His Sermon on the Mount, Jesus was very clear regarding our assessment of other people's lives (see Matthew 7:1 below).

The comforting thing is that there is Someone who does know the most personal and deep details of every step of each person's journey. Read all of Psalm 139 to see and hear just how intimately acquainted God is with each one of us. He knows every trial, every struggle, and every triumph that has made us into who we are. He has the only complete insight on all those issues we struggle with and the effort and, sometimes sweat, it takes to accomplish something that may look completely "seamless" on the outside. Not only does He know how we got to this place—He knows why. Sometimes we are reluctant to tell others those intimate details for fear of losing their love or respect. Truth is, people do not need, or want, to know all the details of our lives. It is different with our heavenly Father, though. Not only does He already know all those things we do not want to reveal to anyone else, He cares about those details and still loves us. In fact, He loves us no matter what, more deeply than any person possibly can, and more than we can possibly fathom.

So, remember that nobody, except the One who created you, knows all the troubles you have seen. He wants, and is able, to help you be victorious over any and in all things that come into your life. May you feel His enormous love for you today and always, Tammy

Tuesday
Scripture: "Do not judge, or you too will be judged." (Matthew 7:1)

Reflect, Activate: Is there one particular thing or things you tend to judge people for? Or is there a person you always feel yourself being judgmental towards? Confess it to the Lord and be forgiven, and then next time your thoughts begin drifting toward judging someone, be aware of it and stop!

Wednesday
Scripture: "But he said to me, 'My grace is sufficient for you, for my power is made perfect in weakness.'" (2 Corinthians 12:9a)

Reflect, Activate: It's difficult to think in terms of great power when our knees are shaking with weakness. What "weakness" do you feel you have that you need to turn over to the Lord?

Thursday
Scripture: "No, despite all these things, overwhelming victory is ours through Christ, who loved us." (Romans 8:37, NLT)

Reflect, Activate: Remember all those movies made about the underdog where it seems there is no way they can win against the stronger team/person/circumstance? They always make us root for the unlikely hero, and it makes us feel good to see them overcome or win. What thing have you struggled with in your life and overcome that no one else would ever know about?

Friday
Scripture: "The righteous cry out, and the Lord hears them; he delivers them from all their troubles. The LORD is close to the brokenhearted and saves those who are crushed in spirit." (Psalm 34:17-18)

Reflect, Activate: What does it mean to be crushed in spirit? How has the Lord helped you when you felt this way or were in some kind of trouble?

Saturday and Sunday
Scripture: "He knows about everyone, everywhere. Everything about us is bare and wide open to the all-seeing eyes of our living God; nothing can be hidden from him to whom we must explain all that we have done." (Hebrews 4:13, NLT)

Reflect, Activate: How does the meaning of this verse change when reading as a non-follower of Christ and then as a follower of Christ?

Prayer for Week: Thank You, Lord, that You know each of us better than we know ourselves and love us in spite of all of our shortcomings. Help me to remember to see others as Your children that You love and care for deeply.

WEEK 15

Can Our Thoughts Be Toxic?

"Finally, brethren, whatever things are true, whatever things are noble, whatever things are just, whatever things are pure, whatever things are lovely, whatever things are of good report, if there is any virtue and if there is anything praiseworthy—meditate on these things." (Philippians 4:8, NKJV)

In the above verse the Bible speaks about dwelling on the good, fine, and lovely things. Did you ever ponder that what we focus on in our thought life releases certain chemicals in our body? A few years ago, I read the book, *Who Switched Off My Brain?* by Dr. Caroline Leaf of South Africa. Dr. Leaf lectures at various secular and Christian conferences on diverse issues relating to optimal brain performance. Her topics include toxic thoughts and strongholds, to name a few. Her book really inspired me to look at and pay attention to what I focus on in my daily thoughts. Could the way I think, either positive or negative, make a difference in whether I enjoy my life or not? Could it also make a difference in my relationships with others or in my spiritual and personal success? After reading Dr. Leaf's book and after much prayer, I would have to say, "Yes! My thoughts can make a difference in all areas of my life!"

I have learned that laughter, along with happy and positive thoughts, releases certain chemicals that elevate our moods. These chemicals can actually help us to heal. Since I have a chronic disability, you can see why I would find it important to pursue anything that could help me to feel better and to be the best that I can be. The Word of God instructs us in Proverbs 17:22 that "a cheerful heart is good medicine." I believe God's Word is like a compass, written to show us directions on how to live a happy, productive life, and also so we can be there for others. So, let's take a minute to look into God's Word and see what He says about bad thoughts and how destructive they can be, not only to ourselves but to those around us.

If "a cheerful heart is good medicine," then what do you suppose bad thoughts, such as unforgiveness or anger or fear, do to our bodies and spirit? These negative strongholds can affect our health and emotional state. If our thoughts are focused on negative things, they will pollute our attitudes toward life and other people. It has been scientifically proven that if we do not deal with these strongholds, they can manifest in an adverse way in our health and how we live.

We have such a health crisis in our country! I am not implying that every health problem is related to bad thoughts. What I am saying is that happier, healthier thoughts can help you to be the best you can be in your current situation. They can help you to better enjoy what you have to work with. We all have pain of one sort or another, whether it is physical or emotional. It is how we deal with it that makes the difference. If you control your thought life by praying and spending time with God through worship and His Word, you will see how much better you feel, and also how that affects those around you.

The good news is this: The Lord can and will help us. Positive thinking is helpful; but by itself, it will not last and will not be enough! We need God's divine intervention to help us experience miracles that only God can do. This is not possible without Him. Only through God can this victory over our thought life be lasting and satisfying. It is through prayer and trusting in God's Word that you will receive the help you need. Our true security is in Him. Without Him, stress and depression can overtake you. Sure, we can go for a while on our own, but true and lasting quality of life is found only in the Lord. We were created to be in fellowship with Him. Without Him, we will fail. To be truly successful, we have to meditate on God's truth.

It takes spiritual power to be a true overcomer, not only in our thought life, but in body, mind, and spirit. If we are leaning on Him, we need not fear—ever! Your thoughts can be in tune with God's thoughts. Ask Him for wisdom in this; make that your goal today.

Have you given thought to where you will be after you have finished your work here on earth? You can receive Jesus into your heart to be the Lord and Savior of your life. If you want assurance of your eternity in heaven, you can pray the sample prayer of salvation on page 3 of this book. Go today and be a blessing in His Name, Iris

Tuesday
Scripture: "We demolish arguments and every pretension that sets itself up against the knowledge of God, and we take captive every thought to make it obedient to Christ." (2 Corinthians 10:5) "For as he thinks in his heart, so is he." (Proverbs 23:7, NKJV)

Reflect, Activate: We all struggle with negative thoughts now and then. What persistent negative thought(s) are you dealing with? Ask God to help you get rid of them.

Wednesday
Scripture: "Do not conform to the pattern of this world, but be transformed by the renewing of your mind. Then you will be able to test and approve what God's will is—his good, pleasing and perfect will." (Romans 12:2)

Reflect, Activate: Think of the all the ways God has transformed your life. Thank Him for the changes you've seen that have made your life better and more joyful.

Thursday
Scripture: "I can do all things through Christ who strengthens me." (Philippians 4:13, NKJV)

Reflect, Activate: What are you facing right now that you need to focus on the promise in this verse? When in the past did the strength of Christ get you through something?

Friday
Scripture: "That if you confess with your mouth, 'Jesus is Lord,' and believe in your heart that God raised him from the dead, you will be saved." (Romans 10:9)

Reflect, Activate: Is there someone you know who needs to hear this truth? Pray for them and ask God to show you how to tell them.

Saturday and Sunday
Scripture: "God is our refuge and strength, an ever-present help in trouble." (Psalms 46:1)

Reflect, Activate: Think about a time in your life that you now know was only God who protected you and gave you the strength to make it through.

Prayer for the Week: Lord Jesus, in this world it is so easy to let the bombardment of the negative around us seep into our thoughts. Help me to be transformed daily by You and to keep my thoughts and words positive and uplifting so that people around me will see You.

WEEK 16

Never Alone, Never Left Out

> "I took you from the ends of the earth, from its farthest corners I called you. I said, 'You are my servant'; I have chosen you and have not rejected you. So do not fear, for I am with you; do not be dismayed, for I am your God. I will strengthen you and help you; I will uphold you with my righteous right hand." (Isaiah 41:9-10)

The neighborhood kids ran down the sidewalk carrying baseball bats and gloves. He stood in the front yard and watched them laughing, doing what friends do, and being 12-year-old boys. He was sure they saw him. How could they not? But they didn't act like it, and they didn't ask him to go with them to the park where there was a game every day after school. He had not played in one. His new glove stood posed on his hand, in plain sight, and ready for an invitation. Left out. Alone. Again.

Do you ever feel this way? Like you are an outcast of a group and not invited to the party? Maybe it is your workplace or school or family. It can even be within the (seemingly) friendly circle of a church congregation. People can make us feel excluded, as if we are not worthy of being included in their "club." The fact is this: unless you are living on some deserted island, this will happen in your human relationships.

However, there is no such thing in the family of God; it is all inclusive. When Jesus came to this earth, He endured many times of being treated like as an outcast. He knows what it feels like (see Isaiah 53:3 below). But here is the good news: if you have made Jesus your Lord and Savior, you are automatically a member of God's "in crowd." You have a place to belong. Always. Forever. There is no better place to be. He came so that gap between us and the Father would be bridged, and we never have to feel as if we are the family member on the outside looking in.

This means that God will never abandon you or pass you by or forget about you. You will never be considered not good enough to be on God's team. Even if you have felt turned aside by the very people you counted on in this life, the Lord will not do that to you.

So, when you do feel left out by people, turn your focus on how much God loves you and that He will never leave your side. What a comfort! If you see someone feeling rejected and alone, do what you can to make them feel included and tell them about how the Lord has helped you in that area. Blessing and Peace in our Lord Jesus Christ, Tammy

Tuesday
Scripture: "He was despised and rejected—a man of sorrows, acquainted with deepest grief. We turned our backs on him and looked the other way. He was despised, and we did not care." (Isaiah 53:3, NLT)

Reflect, Activate: What do you think were the main reasons Jesus was despised while He was here on this earth? Do you think some of them had a change of heart after He was crucified and then rose from the grave?

Wednesday
Scripture: "For his Spirit joins with our spirit to affirm that we are God's children." (Romans 8:16, NLT)

Reflect, Activate: It is almost overwhelming to think about the Maker of all of the universe calling us His children. What do we want the world to see in us to reflect that we are, indeed, His children?

Thursday
Scripture: "Even if my father and mother abandon me, the Lord will hold me close." (Psalm 27:10, NLT)

Reflect, Activate: Perhaps you feel, or have felt, abandoned by people who were supposed to have played a significant role in your life. If so, write this Scripture on your heart (memorize it) and choose to believe He is close to you. Ask the Lord to help you see people around you who feel alone and abandoned and then give them encouragement.

Friday
Scripture: "What, then, shall we say in response to these things? If God is for us, who can be against us? He who did not spare his own Son, but gave him up for us all—how will he not also, along with him, graciously give us all things? For I am convinced that neither death nor life, neither angels nor demons, neither the present nor the future, nor any powers, neither height nor depth, nor anything else in all creation, will be able to separate us from the love of God that is in Christ Jesus our Lord." (Romans 8:31-32, 38-39)

Reflect: What challenge are you facing today? Now think about how God is on your side and that His love is stuck to you! How does this encourage you?

Saturday and Sunday

Scripture: "Keep your lives free from the love of money and be content with what you have, because God has said, 'Never will I leave you; never will I forsake you.'" (Hebrews 13:5)

Reflect, Activate: Write a list of all you are thankful for that God has supplied for you. Look at this list often! It will reinforce how He has never left you.

Prayer for Week: Thank You for Your promise that You will never abandon us or forsake us, no matter what the world throws at us.

WEEK 17

Are We On a Journey? What Is Our Destination?

> "The LORD had said to Abram, 'Leave your country, your people and your father's household and go to the land I will show you.'" (Genesis 12:1)

Have you thought that every journey in life can be about a destination? Well, where are we headed and how do we get there? You are on a journey, orchestrated by God Himself, that no one else can take for you. It is uniquely designed by God for you alone. Each of us can look at our trip through life as a negative thing, or we can view it as the most exciting thing we will ever experience.

Your life is an excursion with God, full of all kinds of adventures along the way into many unknowns. These are the choices we have: we can view it as scary, or we can look at it with anticipation of great and mighty things. Even though only you can navigate your particular journey, there is Someone who can help you along this path. It is God Himself! You are not traveling alone. First find out who God is, then investigate who you are and where you are going. He made you! He knows you intimately and what you are all about. Most comforting is that He knows what you need for the journey ahead.

God called Abram on a journey into the desert (see Genesis 12). He had nothing and did not even know where he was going. He did not know who he was, how he would eat, or where he would sleep. No details were laid out for him when God told him to go. Yet, he trusted God to lead him, guide him, and provide for him. This was a man who truly lived by faith. Because of Abram's faith, God provided everything he needed—not necessarily his wants, but definitely his needs.

Today, we are on a journey similar to Abram's. Even if you do not understand where God has you now, or where you are going, or how you are going to get there, or even what provisions will be made, look up to God! Even if you do not understand anything about the journey that you're on at this time, step toward Him. Then guess what? He will be there for you. God loves you! Our God can take anything and turn it into something good. My friend, you may be facing some hard times right now. The future may seem bleak and uncertain. You ask, "How will this all turn out?" But as I said, God can turn anything into something good.

Are We On a Journey? What Is Our Destination?

Many of the roads we walk in life's journey don't seem to make sense. Why are there so many challenges? Will it ever get better? What is going to happen? Many questions we ask about life can be frightening. Not knowing the results at the end of the road can be unsettling. Where do I go from here? What do I do? What strategy do I take? How can we know for sure what direction to take on our journey? My friend, turn to God, because only He knows the answers for sure! Abram prayed and asked God what direction to take, and God answered him.

Most people today wait until they are at the end of their rope to pray, but you don't have to. How should we pray when we do not understand the journey or even know how to pray? God tells us in the scriptures how to pray (see Matthew 6:9-13 below) Tell Him exactly what is on your heart; pour it out to Him. He hears you and even counts each and every tear you may shed.

What does life hold for you? Ask God what direction you need to take (see Isaiah 30:21 below). Whose voice will you hear? I'm not saying His answers will always be easy. However, the direction He leads you on your journey will be what is best for you and, I am sure, what is best for those around you also. Step toward Him, my friend, and trust that He will step toward you and will answer your prayers.

This reminds me of when I was a little girl and riding in the car with my parents. As I sat in the back seat, I trusted that wherever they took me, it would be good and what was best for me. I had a choice: I could sit quietly trusting, or I could question where we were going and why. It is the same in our life with God. We can try to get in the front seat with Him and help Him drive. This, I am sure, would cause the car to start careening all over the road, and it may possibly crash. We might try to tell Him which way we want to go. This, more than likely, would cause our journey to be longer and harder, and we may not fully live out what God has for us. Or our other option is to trust Him and let Him take us on the best route for the best results. God truly is the best global positioning system.

We often turn to things in life to help ease the stress (eating comfort foods, talking with friends, and other habits). These can take the edge off, but God is the only One who can bring true and lasting peace for the journey we are on. Let Him direct you; He is the only One who will not disappoint you. Yes, life is a journey, and sometimes it will take us to places we do not want to go to experience things we do not want to experience. There are bumps in the road but be encouraged, my friend. When your journey on this earth comes to an end, won't it be wonderful to hear God Himself say: "Well done, good and faithful servant!" That is what we have waiting for us at the end of our journey when we pass from this life into eternity, which is for forever! God's blessings, Iris

Tuesday
Scripture: "Ask and it will be given to you; seek and you will find; knock and the door will be opened to you." (Matthew 7:7)

Reflect, Activate: What do you need direction for today? Pray and ask God to show you what to do.

Wednesday
Scripture: "Call to me and I will answer you and tell you great and unsearchable things you do not know." (Jeremiah 33:3)

Reflect, Activate: Is there a difficult question you need to ask God? It could be something like, "Why did that person die?"

Or "What direction am I supposed to go now in my career?" Approach Him in prayer and see what He has to say.

Thursday
Scripture: "And we know that in all things God works for the good of those who love him, who have been called according to his purpose." (Romans 8:28)

"Well done, good and faithful servant! You have been faithful with a few things; I will put you in charge of many things. Come and share your master's happiness!" (Matthew 25:23)

Reflect, Activate: Can you recall a time in your life or in someone else's when things looked extremely bleak? Perhaps it looked as if there was no possible solution for a problem or struggle. Now, can you look back and see how God worked things out for good?

Friday
Scripture: "This, then, is how you should pray: 'Our Father in heaven, hallowed be your name, your kingdom come, your will be done, on earth as it is in heaven. Give us today our daily bread. And forgive us our debts, as we also have forgiven our debtors. And lead us not into temptation, but deliver us from the evil one.'" (Matthew 6:9-13)

Reflect, Activate: Jesus gave this prayer as a guide for how to pray. But what does it mean? Research it and see. One suggestion is on Christianity.com: https://www.christianity.com/wiki/prayer/breakdown-of-the-lords-prayer.html

Saturday and Sunday
Scriptures: "Come near to God and he will come near to you." (James 4:8a)

"Whether you turn to the right or to the left, your ears will hear a voice behind you, saying, 'This is the way; walk in it.'" (Isaiah 30:21)

Reflect, Activate: God has promised to guide us if we ask Him. Pray and ask Him for direction for something you need guidance in, but then be prepared to listen to what He wants to say to you.

Prayer for Week: Guide me along my journey, Lord, to bring me to my heavenly home with You. Give me direction and comfort when I get to a difficult spot in this life, and help me to constantly keep focused on You and my final destination.

WEEK 18

The Shoulda Beens

"Brothers and sisters, I do not consider myself yet to have taken hold of it. But one thing I do: Forgetting what is behind and straining toward what is ahead, [14] I press on toward the goal to win the prize for which God has called me heavenward in Christ Jesus." (Philippians 3:13-14)

We were not exactly ready for the Pro Bowling Tour. Strikes and spares seemed to elude us—one or two pins were left standing to mock us on a regular basis. "That shoulda been a strike!" we said many times. So, our team became "The Shoulda Beens." It was perfect.

I want to shout out that very same thing some days. There is a real danger, spiritually and emotionally, when we look too much at what should have or could have been instead of what is. This is a battle for me, as I am sure it is for many. The reality is we all have stuff in our yesterdays that can provoke regrets and guilt. Our past does play a role in who we are today; we cannot pretend it does not exist. That would be unrealistic and even somewhat dangerous in some instances. However, there is good news! Jesus is Lord of our past, present, and future. He knows all about our "shoulda beens," and the struggles we have because of them. How comforting to place all our times in His capable hands.

"...forgetting what lies behind..." This word is true and exactly what God wants us to do—to move on. However, it is not always wrong or bad to look back. It can save us from perhaps repeating a past mistake or getting into an abusive situation again. I also believe we are supposed to recall the Lord's faithfulness in the past. Think back on all the times that God came through for you during a challenging circumstance or seemingly impossible situation. Maybe He supplied the money for a necessity, or He filled you with peace when something hurtful or tragic happened. He promises to give us everything we need, when we need it. Thinking about those past times can be such an encouragement for use for the present and future. Telling others about His faithfulness in your past may give someone the hope they need for whatever they are dealing with at that moment.

What He says in His Word we can count on. Period. What a comfort that is! So, we can go forward from all the "shoulda beens," whether those were of our own making, or they were imposed on us from other sources (people or circumstances, etc.). He promises to be with us as we move on. If He carried us through before, we can be sure He will again. Remember—He will never, ever, ever leave you or forsake you. Be in His presence, Tammy

Tuesday
Scripture: "Remember the things I have done in the past. For I alone am God! I am God, and there is none like me." (Isaiah 46:9, NLT)

Reflect, Activate: What has God done for you in the past? Write down a few of them and then commit to telling someone today or this week about one or more of those times.

Wednesday
Scripture: "And my God will meet all your needs according to the riches of his glory in Christ Jesus." (Philippians 4:19)

Reflect, Activate: What do you think "needs" means in this verse? Is it just food, water, shelter? I think it includes emotionally, spiritually, etc. Has the Lord ever supplied that friend just when you needed him/her? Has He ever calmed you frightened heart just when you needed Him to?

Thursday
Scripture: "The grass withers and the flowers fall, but the word of our God endures forever." (Isaiah 40:8)

Reflect, Activate: Think on all the things of this world that are here today and gone tomorrow. Then search for Scripture for the eternal things God promises.

Friday
Scripture: "He has delivered us from such a deadly peril, and he will deliver us again. On him we have set our hope that he will continue to deliver us." (2 Corinthians 1:10)

Reflect, Activate: Think about situations the Lord has delivered you from. How did He do that? Did you realize He was delivering you at the time or was it later when you became aware of what a big deliverance it truly was? Remember that next time it seems as if He is leading you in a direction that makes no sense. Perhaps, He is saving you from something coming down the road.

Saturday and Sunday
Scripture: "I will remember the deeds of the Lord; yes, I will remember your miracles of long ago. I will consider all your works and meditate on all your mighty deeds." Your ways, God, are holy. What god is as great as our God? You are the God who performs miracles; you display your power among the peoples." (Psalm 77:11-14)

Reflect, Activate: Look for some of the "big" deeds God performed in the Old Testament. Think about how some of them seemed pretty ridiculous to the people at the time. Remember— God always has a plan for you!

Prayer for Week: Lord, help me to always remember Your faithfulness to me in the past, knowing that You will also be faithful now and in the future.

WEEK 19

God's Love Stuck in Our Hearts

"For God so loved the world that he gave His one and only Son, that whoever believes in him shall not perish but have eternal life." (John 3:16)

The familiarity of this verse and the frequency in which we have heard it can cause us to gloss over the amazing truth it declares. The implication is clear, and yet, do I really grasp the power behind this passage? Oh, I believe it for everyone else—but for me? That is different. Sure, God loved the world, but does He love me?

Many years ago, a friend told me during a difficult time in my life, "God loves you so much." I did not completely buy it. I wondered—does He really? Even though I was not completely convinced what she said was true, I never forgot it. I went back to it many times over the years and found comfort that maybe, just maybe God does love me. The above verse certainly says so. But comprehension of this wonderful promise may take a long time and can be challenging to fully accept.

God has tenderly and persistently reminded me over the years that He loves me just for who I am. And that He cannot possibly love me any more or any less no matter what I do or say or what has transpired in my past or will happen in the future. Period. He loves us unconditionally. It does not matter what others say or think of me or even what I think about myself. This can be new territory for some of us because the world can be very convincing that love has stipulations. Accepting that God truly loves us without any strings attached can be particularly challenging for people who discover someone has loved them only for their physical beauty, a particular talent, money, or that they somehow don't live up to the expectations of others.

Although my struggle of accepting this truth has lessened over the years, I still sometimes deal with thoughts of—if I mess up, even one time, God may leave me and/or stop loving me. This is just not true, because His character will not allow it. We also have the assurance from His Word, which I have to go back to over and over.

I want to be mindful every day, throughout the day, of God's love for me. He loves me more than I can even hope to comprehend in the feebleness of my human brain. My part is to accept His love for me and to put my trust in Him. One of my favorite verses on this subject is Ephesians 3 (see below).

Isn't it awesome to know that the Maker of the Universe and of everything in it, loves us so completely that He would die for us? Read John 3:16 above over and over until the assurance of God's love gets stuck in your heart. Resting in His Love, Tammy

Tuesday
Scripture: "But make everyone rejoice who puts his trust in you. Keep them shouting for joy because you are defending them. Fill all who love you with your happiness. For you bless the godly man, O Lord; you protect him with your shield of love." (Psalm 5:11-12, NLT)

Reflect, Activate: Picture God's powerful love like a shield standing between you and the world and your struggles. Thank Him for always loving you! Like my friend told me years ago, send someone a message simply telling them how much God loves them.

Wednesday
Scripture: "...because God has said, 'Never will I leave you; never will I forsake you.'" (Hebrews 13:5)

Reflect, Activate: Look up the definition and synonyms of "forsake." Now, think about how this is what God has promised to never, ever do.

Thursday
Scripture: "For this reason I kneel before the Father, from whom every family in heaven and on earth derives its name. I pray that out of his glorious riches he may strengthen you with power through his Spirit in your inner being, so that Christ may dwell

in your hearts through faith. And I pray that you, being rooted and established in love, may have power, together with all the Lord's holy people, to grasp how wide and long and high and deep is the love of Christ, and to know this love that surpasses knowledge—that you may be filled to the measure of all the fullness of God." (Ephesians 3:14-19)

Reflect, Activate: Ponder how the love of Jesus for us is so vast that our human minds cannot even comprehend it. Look up Scriptures that talk about this love, and then let your mind dwell on them.

Friday
Scripture: "This is how we know what love is: Jesus Christ laid down his life for us. And we ought to lay down our lives for our brothers and sisters." (1 John 3:16)

Reflect, Activate: What does it mean to lay down your life for a brother or sister in Christ?

Saturday and Sunday
Scripture: "Your steadfast love, O Lord, is as great as all the heavens. Your faithfulness reaches beyond the clouds. How precious is your constant love, O God! All humanity takes refuge in the shadow of your wings." (Psalm 36:5 & 7, NLT)

Reflect, Activate: The Bible speaks a lot about God's protection on us as His children. Look up verses pertaining to this.

Prayer for Week: Lord, thank You for loving me more than I can possibly fathom. As I remember Your love for me, help me to show others that same love and acceptance.

WEEK 20
What Does God Expect From Us?

> "You shall have no other gods before me. You shall not make for yourself an image in the form of anything in heaven above or on the earth beneath or in the waters below. You shall not bow down to them or worship them; for I, the LORD your God, am a jealous God" (Exodus 20:3-5a)

Originally, in the cool of the evening in the Garden of Eden, God created us to walk with Him.

However, since that time, we have done what we want to do. Throughout His Word, God almost pleads with us to be in a relationship with Him and obey His commandments (see Deuteronomy 6:10-17 below).

My friends, consider where you are with the Lord right now. Do you love Him, or do you love the provisions He brings? It reminds me of a child who gets great gifts from his parents, but the parents never teach the child to love them alone and not the gifts that they are giving him. The child becomes spoiled and even demanding to the point that when the provision is gone, the child is no longer faithful to the parents. He did not learn to love them for who they are, not just for what he could get from them. Isn't this some of what we see in our society today? Let me take you back in time for a moment. Before World War II, there was a time of great rebellion. Then during the Great Depression, many people were so broken they repented and turned back to God. After the war God blessed our nation for that repentance. But what has happened? After decades of blessings, many people have forgotten God again, haven't they?

Today, you may be in the middle of a trial. Pray and consider what is God trying to say to you. Have you forgotten the One who brought you into such tremendous blessings? Do you love the gift more than the giver? Remember, my friend, God loves you, and He created you for His fellowship. He does want to give us all good things, but where is your relationship with Him today? Have your possessions become what you worship more? Remember, we do serve a jealous God, and He will have no other gods before Him. I don't mean to sound harsh, but all God wants is for us to walk with Him. Give Him your all (your time, your money, your heart, your life), and watch what He will do. Anything that takes the place of God in our lives is idolatry (see Exodus at top of page).

So, what does God expect from us? It's simple. He expects us to take time to fellowship with Him and love Him; that's all. If you choose to do this and put Him first, the things you desire most will follow. Will you walk with Him today? Have you received Jesus into your heart to be the Lord and Savior of your life? If not, you can pray the prayer of salvation. There are examples on page 3 of this devotional.

Bless you, my friend, Iris

Tuesday
Scripture: "When the LORD your God brings you into the land he swore to your fathers, to Abraham, Isaac and Jacob, to give you—a land with large, flourishing cities you did not build, houses filled with all kinds of good things you did not provide, wells you did not dig, and vineyards and olive groves you did not plant—then when you eat and are satisfied, be careful that you do not forget the LORD, who brought you out of Egypt,

out of the land of slavery. Fear the LORD your God, serve him only and take your oaths in his name. Do not follow other gods, the gods of the peoples around you; for the LORD your God, who is among you, is a jealous God and His anger will burn against you, and he will destroy you from the face of the land. Do not test the LORD your God as you did at Massah. Be sure to keep the commands of the LORD your God and the stipulations and decrees he has given you. (Deuteronomy 6:10-17)

Reflect, Activate: Take time today to think about (and maybe even write down) all the blessings God has given you.

Wednesday
Scripture: "'Bring the whole tithe into the storehouse, that there may be food in My house. Test Me in this,' says the LORD Almighty, 'and see if I will not throw open the floodgates of heaven and pour out so much blessing that you will not have room enough for it.'" (Malachi 3:10)

Reflect, Activate: How have you seen God bless your life as a result of tithing? Or giving money, time, or some other resource to others?

Thursday
Scripture: "For they provoked Him to anger with their high places, and moved Him to jealousy with their carved images." (Psalms 78:58, NKJV)

Reflect, Activate: Many things can be "gods" in our lives – money, relationships, a job. These are not bad in and of themselves, but the importance we put on them can be a problem. Have there been times (or now) when something other than

God has been the focus of your life? Ask Him to help you put things back into perspective in a way that pleases Him.

Friday
Scripture: "I can do all this through him who gives me strength." (Philippians 4:13)

Reflect, Activate: What do you need Christ's strength for right now? Allow Him to use His strength in that area of your life.

Saturday and Sunday
Scripture: "One of them, an expert in the law, tested him with this question: 'Teacher, which is the greatest commandment in the Law?' Jesus replied: 'Love the Lord your God with all your heart and with all your soul and with all your mind. This is the first and greatest commandment. And the second is like it: 'Love your neighbor as yourself.' All the Law and the Prophets hang on these two commandments.'" (Matthew 22:35-40)

Reflect, Activate: Why do you think Jesus said these two commandments were the most important? Reflect on who your "neighbor" is.

Prayer for the Week: Lord, thank You that You love us so deeply and want to be in fellowship with us. Help me to be mindful of Your presence at all times and to not have any other "gods" before You. Thank You for all the blessings You have given to me and to those around me. In Jesus' Name, Amen.

WEEK 21

The Great Provider

> "And my God shall supply all your need according to His riches in glory by Christ Jesus." (Philippians 4:19, NKJV)

God will provide. I know that. I believe that. Or do I? If obtaining the necessities of life became difficult, would I completely trust God to take care of my family and me in every way? Honestly, I do not know, because I have never been in that position. However, I do know someone who has.

I met Margaret when we lived just a couple of blocks from each other. She did not have a phone at the time, so the church we both attended called me one day to relay a message to her. So began a friendship that has lasted for over 30 years (and counting)—through many trying times for each of us. This precious lady taught me the true meaning of trusting God for every need no matter what the circumstances look like.

Margaret was a single mom with four children, one who had critical health issues requiring expensive medicine and treatment. I saw her work from early morning until late at night to provide for herself and her kids. There was not extra of anything—ever. Unless, of course, you count struggles and hard times, because she sure had her share of those.

I remember her telling me how many times throughout her life she did not know where their next meal was coming from or if they would have a place to live in the future. The car she had for a while had brakes that barely worked. She had to get to work, so there was no choice but to get in and drive. She prayed every time she took the car out, and God protected her. I have never had to worry about any of those issues. Even now, my heart still breaks for her for all she has gone through.

Isn't it amazing how God puts people in our lives to show us His Word in action? It is easy to read or hear a scripture and nod our heads in agreement while shouting, "You preach it, brother! Amen, sister! Hallelujah!" But it is a whole different thing to watch someone trust what God says in His Word for a real-life situation and then witness the fulfillment of that promise in their life. Our own faith is strengthened. We realize that if He provided for the other person, then He will provide for us, too.

I thank God for bringing Margaret into my life to be a sister in Christ and to help me trust in His promise of provision. She faced overwhelming circumstances at times; some of them were frightening. I observed how she handled whatever came her way, and this is what I saw: God supplied the food, shelter, and protection she needed. Provision also came for her faith to stay strong. Sometimes the need was fulfilled at the last minute, but

He never EVER failed her or her family. Thanking Him for all His provisions, Tammy

Tuesday
Scripture: "So don't worry about these things, saying, 'What will we eat? What will we drink? What will we wear?' These things dominate the thoughts of unbelievers, but your heavenly Father already knows all your needs. Seek the Kingdom of God above all else, and live righteously, and he will give you everything you need. So don't worry about tomorrow, for tomorrow will bring its own worries. Today's trouble is enough for today." (Matthew 6:31-34, NLT)

Reflect, Activate: Have you ever found yourself desperate for some physical or emotional need? How did God fulfill that need? If you have a need right now, trust Him completely to take care of you!

Wednesday
Scripture: "He who did not spare his own Son, but gave him up for us all—how will he not also, along with him, graciously give us all things?" (Romans 8:32)

Reflect, Activate: Make a list of all God has given you. Thank Him and then remember this as you face your next challenge.

Thursday
Scripture: "And God is able to bless you abundantly, so that in all things at all times, having all that you need, you will abound in every good work." (2 Corinthian 9:8)

Reflect, Activate: Look around and see what you may have an abundance of (clothes, food, etc.). Then find someone or some place you can give these things to so others are blessed.

Friday
Scripture: "Consider the ravens: They do not sow or reap, they have no storeroom or barn; yet God feeds them. And how much more valuable you are than birds!" (Luke 12:24)

Reflect, Activate: Read other accounts about God's provision to His children. For example: the manna in the desert He provided for the Israelites (Exodus 16) or Elijah and the widow (1 Kings 17).

Saturday and Sunday
Scripture: "If you then, being evil, know how to give good gifts to your children, how much more will your Father who is in heaven give good things to those who ask Him!" (Matthew 7:11, NKJV)

Reflect, Activate: Think about what it feels like when you give a gift to someone—something they need or want. Then think about how much God loves to give us all good things.

Prayer for Week: Lord, help me to remember that You will always give me everything I need, when I need it. Thank You for being the Great Provider.

WEEK 22

What Makes You Afraid?

"For God has not given us a spirit of fear, but of power and of love and of a sound mind." (2 Timothy 1:7, NKJV)

Did you know that being afraid is a normal part of life? There is so much that we do not have control over. Fear is the uncertainty of future events, of not knowing what is going to happen next or the mysterious unknown. How will things turn out? What if I don't make it? God promises us that His goodness and love will follow us all the days of our life (see Psalms 23:6). So, what is there to be afraid of? The Bible assures us that, with Him, nothing can stand up against us.

Faith, on the other hand, is being certain of what we cannot see. That is, no matter what the outcome, even if we were to die, we need not fear. Isn't it nice to know that whatever happens, if we know Jesus, we need never be afraid? In the Bible it says many times to "fear not." For example, in Joshua 1:2, after the death of Moses, God commanded Joshua to lead the Israelites across the Jordan River into the land He wanted to give them. What a challenge for Joshua to assume the responsibility of Moses, one of the greatest leaders of all time. Because the task was beyond his natural ability, fear crept in. However, along with the commandment, God brought comfort to Joshua's heavy heart and encouraged him by promising that He would never leave him. If God commanded Joshua not to fear, there must have been reasons in the natural to be afraid. However, no matter how scary things seemed, Joshua and the people knew they had God with them.

A few years ago, God called me to speak publicly for the first time. Because of all the difficulties I have due to my condition, I lacked confidence in my speaking ability. So, as I prepared for this, fear crept in. All kinds of thoughts plummeted my mind: "What if I don't make sense?", "What if I'm misunderstood?", or "What if I look foolish?" It went on and on! Have you ever felt like the enemy was working you over on some issue? Give it a rest already! Well, anyway, I prayed and moved forward with much apprehension. I kept recalling all the scriptures I could to help me. Then as I stepped out onto the platform, the fear suddenly lifted, and I was able to speak very eloquently. Take note, though, that God did not lift the fear until I had made that first step. As He promised, I had exactly what I needed for what He had called me to do. He gave me peace and clarity of mind. He also gave me the message He wanted to deliver through me as His vessel. So, whatever it is that is making you feel so fearful today, try stepping out in faith as Peter did (see Matthew 14:29-31 below).

Peter was able to walk on the water, as long as he kept his eyes on the Lord, but as soon as he looked at the storm around him, he began to sink. So, whatever "storm" you are facing today that threatens to capsize your life (your health, your finances, a relationship, etc.), walk toward Jesus, looking directly to Him with your shield of faith up. If we lower that shield, the enemy can cause us to doubt God. Then we feel like God did not come through for us when it really was us (you and me) who dropped our shield of faith. God did not move; He is always there. Never forget God's Word, because it is powerful. Do not be tempted to distrust God. He is more than able to help us do anything. My friend, everything that concerns you is under God's care.

Do not stop praying and do keep pressing on. You will be surprised at how well you do. I always have been!

Is there some area of your life or a fear you are tempted not to trust God with? Have you ever thought that this might be the very area He has entrusted to you and wants to use you in the most? Sometimes God trusts us more than we trust Him. So, move on toward what makes you so afraid. Watch Him show off what He can do through you. Trust Him to help you and hear Him say, "See, I knew you could do it!" God responds to our praises and is so blessed when we walk by faith, even if we are afraid.

One final thought: fear distorts our memory of past victories. Our needs are met for today. Sure, it seems scary sometimes, but get a hold of fear or it can control your life. Don't let it! It perverts your past, paralyzes your present, and plunders your future. It does not need to; God is greater than anything you may fear. You truly can do everything God asks you to. You can trust Him. Just ask and see what He will do. My blessings to you, Iris

Tuesday
Scripture: "What, then, shall we say in response to these things? If God is for us, who can be against us?" (Romans 8:31)

Reflect, Activate: Sometimes it can feel as if all is against us. Think back on a time when it seemed like everyone/everything was against you, but now you can see that God was right there with you.

Wednesday
Scripture: "For to me, to live is Christ and to die is gain." (Philippians 1:21)

Reflect, Activate: Many followers of Christ over the years have died because of their beliefs. What are the tangible things we can do while still living here on earth to show people who Jesus is?

Thursday

Scripture: "No one will be able to stand against you all the days of your life. As I was with Moses, so I will be with you; I will never leave you nor forsake you. Have I not commanded you? Be strong and courageous. Do not be afraid; do not be discouraged, for the LORD your God will be with you wherever you go." (Joshua 1:5, 9)

Reflect, Activate: Search for verses in God's Word that talk about not being afraid but being courageous. Write them down, and go to them the next time you need a boost of courage.

Friday

Scripture: "'Come,' he said. Then Peter got down out of the boat, walked on the water and came toward Jesus. But when he saw the wind, he was afraid and, beginning to sink, cried out, 'Lord, save me!' Immediately Jesus reached out his hand and caught him. 'You of little faith,' he said, 'why did you doubt?'" (Matthew 14:29-31)

Reflect, Activate: Think about what it means that Jesus immediately saved Peter from sinking into the abyss. What he did not do was to tell Peter he first had to get his life together before he could be saved. Is there something in your life that keeps you from turning to Jesus and asking for His help? Call out to Him now! He will help you.

Saturday and Sunday
Scriptures: "Jesus looked at them and said, 'With man this is impossible, but with God all things are possible.'" (Matthew 19:26)

"You, dear children, are from God and have overcome them, because the one who is in you is greater than the one who is in the world." (1 John 4:4)

Reflect, Activate: What situation are you facing right now that seems impossible? Read Matthew 19:26 over and over until your heart believes that nothing is impossible with God. Think back on a situation in your life that seemed impossible. How did God work it out? How did your faith grow through that? Tell others about what He has done for you!

Prayer for the Week: Lord Jesus, thank You for the faith and courage You give me, for I know even those things come from You. Help me in this situation I find myself in now, which, through worldly eyes, seems hopeless. I trust in You to bring about a resolution and that Your goodness will come from something that looks completely bad.

WEEK 23

Daily Healings and Miracles

"For he will order his angels to protect you wherever you go."
(Psalm 91:11, NLT)

I believe in big miracles and healings—those of the "Parting of the Red Sea" magnitude. I've heard testimonies of cancer there one check-up and gone the next. They happen, and I know it is the Maker of the Universe who brings them about.

But have you ever thought about all the less noticeable healings that have taken place in your life or have happened to people around you? I remember dealing with colds and the flu and various bruises and scrapes when my three boys were growing up. Of course, I prayed for God to heal them. However, when recovery came, I'm not sure I recognized it for what it really was. Those restorations to health were all miracles of healings, and not necessarily small ones. That cold could have gone into something more serious like pneumonia. Minor injuries could have morphed into a more critical condition.

Then there are the happenings in a so-called normal day that go unrecognized as miracles. For example: what about that mom who goes to the grocery store with four young children in tow and all the kids actually behave? When she gets to the check-out line, there is not a single "surprise" item going down the belt. No colorful words passed out of their little mouths in embarrassing fashion. She sees an elderly neighbor who whispers in her ear, "You are such a good mom." Perhaps her fragile emotions and her mommy confidence received the boost she needed to go on. Now, that's a miracle!

I grew up on a ranch 15 miles from a small town. The houses along the road to our house were miles apart. Late one night when I was a teenager, the engine blew up in the car I was riding in with a friend. It was 20-some below that night, and the highway was deserted with no houses in sight. There was no way we could walk to get help because of the dangerously frigid temperature. We could not sit in the car—it was full of smoke. And of course, there were no cell phones. Within five or ten minutes some people we knew came along and picked us up. I did not know much about God then, and I may have viewed the whole thing as "luck" at the time. But after turning my life over to Jesus, I looked back on that night differently. Not one part of the incident was happenstance. It was the Lord who gave us a miracle and kept us safe that night.

What about instances in your life when you received those seemingly little (but not necessarily insignificant) miracles and/or healings? Try writing them down and then ponder how God has orchestrated a restoration—big or small—in your life or in the lives of the people you know. He takes care of us in so many ways—ways we don't even realize sometimes. Thank Him and trust Him for similar help in the future. He is faithful and He loves you. May God bless you abundantly! Tammy

Tuesday
Scripture: "This is what the LORD, the God of your father David, says: 'I have heard your prayer and seen your tears; I will heal you.'" (2 Kings 20:5)

Reflect, Activate: God sees your tears! If you are facing a difficult situation right now – pray to Him and ask for restoration. Cry if you need to; He knows your heart and what you need.

Wednesday
Scripture: "God is our refuge and strength, an ever-present help in trouble." (Psalm 46:1)

Reflect, Activate: Think about a situation when you needed God's help immediately. How did He help you? Maybe you didn't even recognize it at the time, so thank Him now. The next time you are in a desperate situation, remember how He came to your aid before and know He will do it again.

Thursday
Scripture: "My God is my rock, in whom I take refuge, my shield and the horn of my salvation. He is my stronghold, my refuge and my savior—from violent people you save me. "I called to the LORD, who is worthy of praise, and have been saved from my enemies." (2 Samuel 22:3-4)

Reflect, Activate: How has Jesus saved you from your enemies? Remember enemies don't have to be in the context of war—they may be an addiction, a difficult relationship, or a trying work environment. Was there ever a time when you were spared from actual violence of some sort?

Friday
Scripture: "He will not let your foot slip—he who watches over you will not slumber; indeed, he who watches over Israel will neither slumber nor sleep. The LORD watches over you—the LORD is your shade at your right hand; the sun will not harm you by day, nor the moon by night." (Psalm 121:3-6)

Reflect, Activate: Focus on this—God never sleeps. So, while you are slumbering, He is ever watching over you. As you go to sleep tonight, take comfort in knowing your heavenly Father is awake and on duty.

Saturday and Sunday
Scripture: "The LORD will keep you from all harm—he will watch over your life; the LORD will watch over your coming and going both now and forevermore." (Psalm 121:7-8)

Reflect, Activate: What do you think it means by "The Lord will guard your going out and your coming in…"?

Prayer for Week: Lord, thank You for protecting me even when I didn't yet know You and for all the big and small miracles You have performed in my life.

WEEK 24

Delivered in the Fire

"But he said to me, 'My grace is sufficient for you, for my power is made perfect in weakness.'" (2 Corinthians 12:9a)

A lot of people have prayed for my healing many times. The outcome was not always exactly what I expected or wanted. However, each time I came away with a new measure of grace, peace, stamina, and perhaps, a new revelation and purpose for what God had called me to do. The Lord was doing some great, though challenging, things that I was not always aware of. Even though I could not see His hand at work with my natural eyes, my faith was being built up.

Recently a friend of mine said, "If the painful encounter is still present, you can be delivered in the fire, if not from it." I greatly benefited from hearing this concerning the breakthroughs all of us are trusting God for. Allow me to elaborate: There is a lot of controversy among believers about how to pray and what to pray for, especially when we are faced with tough times and hard situations. The Bible says we must pray believing (see Mark 11:24 below). It is that simple!

So, why is it that sometimes it seems our prayers are not being heard or getting answered in the way we expect? Well, the answer, I believe, is in the Scriptures. Jesus demonstrated the ultimate "giving over to the Father" right before He made the ultimate sacrifice on the cross.

I'll be honest, each time I was prayed for, I had an openness for what God wanted to do in my life along with an intense desire to be healed. I prayed, knowing that God could do it. As I said before, I did come away with a new perspective. Sometimes, I felt a bit better and maybe even was delivered from something so serious it could have taken my life. Still, the illness remained. Did God not hear me? Or did He give me what I needed at that moment to be inspired and strengthened for the work He called me to do? Look at the apostle Paul in 2 Corinthians 12 when he asked God to remove his thorn in the flesh.

You see, the weaker we are, the stronger He can be through us, and the better He can use us. Then there is less of us and more and more of Him, and we do not get in the way of what God is trying to do. Have you ever thought that when we are strong and healthy and everything is going our way that we lean less on Him and more on our own strength? We tend to have less time for God's work and more time for what we think we need—like more money, taking one more vacation, a new relationship, or staying busy to feel more significant.

Does any of this sound familiar? Well, it may be because it is human nature! Our natural tendency is to be selfish. We come out of the womb needy and self-centered, and without God carefully molding us to be more like Him, we gravitate more and more towards self and not particularly toward others. How does this tie in with why some people have more trials and health problems than others? Let me encourage you, my friend: Even if you have great trials or a debilitating illness, God can use you to do awesome things you thought were not possible. Remember, that whatever He has called you to suffer in, He also provides all the grace you will need to maintain.

If you have not been delivered from the fire yet, focus on being delivered in the fire for as long as the LORD has you there. In the Old Testament, Shadrach, Meshach, and Abednego were ordered to go into an extremely hot and fiery furnace. They went in alone. However, a fourth person, whom some believe to have been Jesus, was seen walking in the fire with them. They came out untouched, not burned at all, and with a mighty testimony of God's power and you can, too! (See Daniel 3) When we go through our own trials, we are not alone. As Jesus was with them in the fire, so He is with us in our own fiery trials. He will always sufficiently equip you for the task He has called you to do.

So, what happens when we are prayed for? Sometimes God wants to do something deeper in us spiritually to move us to the next level. It is not always about what we want, and it may not even be for total healing. Rather, it may be to change our hearts. We have a new acceptance of the situation, and how we can be a blessing to others. If we must remain in the circumstance, what better outcome than to be in the center of God's will? There is no better place to be! When you feel like you have to have something right now, God may delay it coming to pass until you are content where you are. God is always up to something good. I am convinced that even if we cannot always see His hand, we can always trust His heart.

I want to encourage you. You can find joy and contentment in helping others, even while experiencing your own "fire." There's tremendous fulfillment in this. It is a joyful blessing to be the answer to someone else's need. The happiest and most content people I know are the ones who help others.

Here are some recommendations to live a more fruitful and productive life: focus on God's blessings in your life, help others, and have an outward giving nature. Embrace where He has you right now as a gift of how mightily He will use you in ways you have never imagined. Let God mold you into the person He desires for you to be: loving, forgiving, and giving. Turn your life over to Him, and watch Him work in your heart and life! Go today and be a blessing in His Name, Iris.

Tuesday
Scripture: "Therefore I tell you, whatever you ask for in prayer, believe that you have received it, and it will be yours." (Mark 11:24)

Reflect, Activate: This can be difficult because we may have prayed for something and not yet received it. Remember that God knows what is best for you because He love you so much! He will bring us peace and comfort, even when the answer to our prayers is no. Perhaps the answer is yes, but the time is not yet come to pass. So, whatever you are praying for today, keep praying and trusting Him.

Wednesday
Scripture: "He went away a second time and prayed, 'My Father, if it is not possible for this cup to be taken away unless I drink it, may your will be done.'" (Matthew 26:42)

Reflect, Activate: Think about a time in your life when you were absolutely certain of what an outcome of a situation should be. Yet, God did something different, and the outcome might have even been the opposite of what you envisioned. Can you see now how His plan did work out for the best?

Thursday
Scripture: "And my God will meet all your needs according to the riches of his glory in Christ Jesus." (Philippians 4:19)

Reflect, Activate: What are your needs today? Are they for your finances or health? Perhaps you need a place to live or food. Maybe you are struggling with a difficult or broken relationship or some emotional or mental troubles. Lean on the above promise from God and ask Him for those needs.

Friday
Scripture: "I am not saying this because I am in need, for I have learned to be content whatever the circumstances." (Philippians 4:11)

Reflect, Activate: Think of a time when your circumstances were not the best. Did you lean on God to help you be content during that difficult time? How have you learned to let God bring you peace when things are tough?

Saturday and Sunday
Scripture: "...for it is God who works in you to will and to act according to his good purpose. Do everything without complaining or arguing." (Philippians 2:13-14)

Reflect, Activate: Here something to try: make a conscious decision to not complain or argue about anything for an hour, a day, or even a week. Watch and see how it affects your attitude and life.

Prayer for Week: Lord Jesus, I know You know best for me. Help me to get out of the way and let You work all things out for the best, not only for me but those around me. Show me how to be content in whatever circumstances I find myself in, knowing You are right there with me.

WEEK 25

All Around Me

"...fixing our eyes on Jesus, the pioneer and perfecter of faith. For the joy set before him he endured the cross, scorning its shame, and sat down at the right hand of the throne of God." (Hebrews 12:2)

There was Moses and the parting of the Red Sea. David brought down Goliath the giant with just a slingshot and a rock. Jesus raised Lazarus from the dead. All were accomplished by the power of God when it looked hopeless because of not-so-good "news." That same power is available today to help us navigate in a world that can easily sidetrack us with negativity and storms. God is in the business of helping His children when it seems as if we are living in a sea of gloom and doom.

I used to get up and be at the gym by 6 a.m. to work out before work. During certain times of the year, the sun was just coming up with glorious colors filling the eastern sky. All was quiet and serene. Then I walked into the building. The world greeted me—very rudely I might add. Music designed to get your blood pumping along with your work-out blared in the background. Multiple televisions hung in front of the cardiac exercise machine with various morning programs on, but mostly the news. Quite a few people were already there, believe it or not, but I did not know anyone. That was okay, because I preferred not to reveal any exercise intolerance I had away from the eyes of friends and family. I had to choose a treadmill positioned in sight of a program I could tolerate—like HGTV or The Travel Channel—a screen not telling me of the state the world was in at the moment. Therefore, all news channels had to be avoided.

I put my ear buds in and listened to music to get my mind set in the right direction for the day. The images and words captioned on the TVs told of a world falling apart and of people who are filled with hopelessness and self-destruction. Maybe an occasional uplifting story would come on, but it was mostly negative and disheartening. However, I had a choice. I could choose to listen to a different message—God's words of assurance of His love for me and the peace He can give me, even in while in turmoil. I wondered if anyone there around me in that building was aware of this alternate message of good news, one contradictory to what society mostly tells us.

What does it mean to fix our eyes on Jesus as it is says in Hebrews 12:2? (See above.) I would describe it as setting my focus on Him and trusting Him no matter what is going on in the world or our lives. This does not mean we ignore all the turmoil and say it is not happening. That would be naïve and a lie. However, if we are only looking at the storms around us, we will not be able to hear the voice of God. His goodness and promises will be drowned out by the clamor of the world and all the noise that brings despair. Romans 8:37-29 (see below) is one verse that helps me the regain the right focus.

What a comfort for this time we are living in! I cannot control what happens around me. However, I can choose to turn my concentration away from all negative words and actions. Then I need to look to Jesus and His promises and not the things of this world undeserving of my attention. Those "things" can be like spoiled children—the more attention you give to them, the more attention they demand and feel entitled to receiving.

So, be encouraged because God is still in control, and He loves you so very much! He longs to help you through any distress you are experiencing personally and to deal with all the trouble in the world. He will give you peace no matter what is going on around you, just simply ask Him. Stay encouraged in Him, Tammy

Tuesday
Scripture: "If then you were raised with Christ, seek those things which are above, where Christ is, sitting at the right hand of God. Set your mind on things above, not on things on the earth." (Colossians 3:1-2, NKJV)

Reflect, Activate: Focusing on Jesus while living in this world can be challenging. Today, make a conscious decision to steer your mind away from the world and onto Him. At the end of the day, look back and see how doing this changed your attitude when you met difficult situations.

Wednesday
Scripture: "He will keep in perfect peace all those who trust in him, whose thoughts turn often to the Lord! Trust in the Lord God always, for in the Lord Jehovah is your everlasting strength." (Isaiah 26:3-4, NLT)

Reflect, Activate: How have you experienced the connection between trusting God and the peace and strength that brings? Can you think of a time when you decided to not trust Him? How was that different?

Thursday
Scripture: "They will have no fear of bad news; their hearts are steadfast, trusting in the LORD." (Psalm 112:7)

Reflect, Activate: What is the definition of steadfast? Then how is that connected to not fearing bad news? Is there something you are fearing might happen in the future? Pray to God and tell Him about your fear and allow Him to help you to not have that fear.

Friday
Scripture: "I have told you these things, so that in me you may have peace. In this world you will have trouble. But take heart! I have overcome the world." (John 16:33)

Reflect, Activate: How does it help you to have peace in the middle of trials when you know the Savior who lives in you has overcome the world? Think about the opposite—how would it be to live in this world with all its troubles without Jesus?

Saturday and Sunday
Scripture: "No, in all these things we are more than conquerors through him who loved us. For I am convinced that neither death nor life, neither angels nor demons, neither the present nor the future, nor any powers, neither height nor depth, nor anything else in all creation, will be able to separate us from the love of God that is in Christ Jesus our Lord." (Romans 8:37-39)

Reflect, Activate: Look up other Scripture that reiterates what this verse says and how there is nothing that can separate us from God.

Prayer for Week: Lord, no matter what storms are going on in my life or this world, I know that Your love and peace will carry me through. Help me to keep my eyes focused on You and not on things that will deter me from You.

WEEK 26

What Are You Passionate About?

"Everything is possible for him who believes." (Mark 9:23)

What are you passionate about? What excites you? When you were a child, do you remember dreaming about what you wanted to be when you grew up? God put these passions and desires in your heart even when you were young, because He wants you to develop them and use them. What better way to glorify God than to use our talents and desires for Him? You will be good at whatever gifts He has given you, because He has already equipped you to be the best you can be.

There will be difficulties in life, and we need to recognize these and deal with them. Good times and bad times will come, but the Lord can use our talents all the time. Focusing on our passions and gifts is important to God. He wants us to enjoy the good times and our gifts, as well as to learn from the hard times. We will grow into prosperity to be used for His glory. You see, suffering brings its own rewards; it strengthens us and gives us His perspective on the direction He wants us to take. That is why the hardships are such an important part of our lives. They make the good and prosperous times so much richer for us.

Finding joy in every situation is a gift: a baby smiling, the sun shining, flowers blooming, etc. These all bring joy. But being passionate about something is different. Finding a passion and using it for the Lord is a joy in itself. For example, if you are a musician or a poet or an athlete, how can you develop and use those talents to glorify God and help others? Even just enjoying the passion for yourself can be glorifying to God. He has given you talents and interests to bless you. He loves you!

Even when obstacles come in life, stay passionate! You can use these obstacles to become greater and stronger and more passionate than ever. This brings joy! God has you in the palm of His hand. It is always easy to get focused on our problems. But instead of magnifying the problem, try magnifying our great big God and the passion He has placed in your heart. The bigger we make God, the smaller our problems become, and the more faith will arise in our hearts.

You may have had disappointments in the past, but this is a new day, a new beginning. Let the past be the past. What are your dreams? Say, "I'm going to get a new vision and victory for the dreams I dreamed so long ago. With God's help and my determination, those dreams will become a reality." Believe it, God still has great things in store for you. Do not live in guilt and condemnation because of past failures. Do not look back like Lot's wife did (see Genesis 19:26 below).

As you get that new vision for your life, let it start inside you. If you can conceive it on the inside, God can bring it to pass on the outside. It is easy to get stuck in a rut. You may think you will never get out of the pain you are in right now, whether it is something physical, a difficult relationship in your life, your job, or finances. You could be thinking, "I'll never see my marriage restored. I'll never get out of debt. I'll never stop hurting." Well, who told you that? Remember, God can do anything. He created the whole universe. Why not get a bigger vision for your life? Go with the passions and dreams you dreamed so long ago. Believe God, the Maker of heaven and earth, to bring them to pass. Now can be a new beginning for you—perhaps to advance your career or to see your talents and gifts come out in a new way.

I believe every one of us has much more in us then we realize. Yes, we all have limitations, but why not let your gifts and talents shine through those limitations and be turned into opportunities for you and for others around you?

I wanted to do something for God, something that mattered. But when I was diagnosed with Celiac disease several years ago, it brought many limitations. What I have done in ministry in these last few years, I never dreamed I would have the energy and strength or joy again to accomplish. Now I have been able to live out many of the dreams I had deep down in myself. I began to serve God with all my heart, weathered many storms, and watched God give me the things I desired most. God is so good!

God will take you places you never ever imagined, which is a testimony in itself. He has a great plan for your life, just like He does for mine. Believe Him for those dreams and passions. You have a purpose; He has given you a specific assignment. There is something He wants you to accomplish through your gifts and dreams.

So, what gifts and talents do you have? Only you and God know! It is easy to get pushed down in life and say, "Oh, I've gone as far as I can. I'm not that great." There's a pity party for you! Do not believe it. You have far more to offer than you think. God has planted seeds of greatness in you, and He wants to accomplish great things through you. He is the one who has breathed life into you and is on your side. You are a person of destiny. God does not want us to be at the same place next year as we are now. Do you? Get a vision that you are going to be more passionate about your life and come up much higher in spite of challenges, weaknesses, and obstacles. You can do it!

Another thought: Do you believe you have favor with God? Regardless of the economy or whatever is going on in our world,

God is in control. He will help us to overcome. Challenges are a part of life. Everyone has experienced challenges and negative things at one time or another in his/her life, but God promises to bring us to a better place than before. Keep smiling; good things are in store for you. Do not wait for "someday" to be happy—today is the day. Life goes by so fast, and every day is a gift from God. Dream big dreams, my friend. It is all good! Even if you do not feel well physically, choose to enjoy each day just the way you are and be the best you can be. Make the most of every opportunity. The enemy wants our joy; do not let him have it. What kind of a testimony is it to the world if we, as Christians, walk around all defeated and discouraged? Happiness is a choice! This world needs more happy people and fewer difficult people. Which one will you be? That is why I like going to church. I love to be around all the praise and joy. I hope you do, too! Iris

Tuesday
Scripture: "But Lot's wife looked back, and she became a pillar of salt." (Genesis 19:26)

Reflect, Activate: Is there something in your past you continually revisit that is causing you distress? It is time to leave it in the past, put it into Jesus' hands, and move forward. If you need to, write it on a piece of paper and pray that you are able to give it up to Him. Then rip it up with great fanfare!

Wednesday
Scripture: "If God is for us, who can ever be against us?" (Romans 8:31b, NLT)

Reflect, Activate: Focus on this – the God who made the universe and everything in it, including you, is on your team. We cannot possibly lose if He is on our side, and He is. Hallelujah!

Thursday
Scripture: "The path of the righteous is like the morning sun, shining ever brighter till the full light of day." (Proverbs 4:18,)

Reflect, Activate: Decide to be a light in the darkness of this world. If you go into a store, smile at a worker. Call someone or send a card just to say you were thinking of them. People need to see the light of Jesus!

Friday
Scriptures: "This is the day the LORD has made; let us rejoice and be glad in it." (Psalms 118:24)

"You will show me the path of life; in Your presence is fullness of joy; at Your right hand are pleasures forevermore. (Psalms 16:11, NKJV)

Reflect, Activate: Think of the things in your life you find joy in. Thank the Lord for those little, or not so little things. Think of a way you can bring that joy to someone else today.

Saturday and Sunday
Scripture: "I have told you these things, so that in me you may have peace. In this world you will have trouble. But take heart! I have overcome the world." (John 16:33)

Reflect, Activate: If you are troubled today, remember where and with whom you can find true peace. Reach out to Jesus and rest in Him!

Prayer for Week: Lord, thank You for the joy You bring us even when things are difficult. Show me how I can be Your light in the world and to someone personally.

WEEK 27

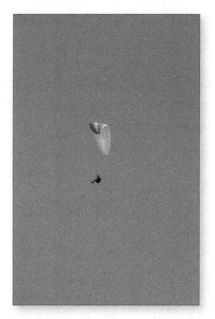

Knowing Him in the Great Alone

"You hem me in behind and before, and you lay your hand upon me." (Psalm 139:5)

This is my friend, Susan's, story as she told it to me:
I was alone in the room. No one could come in with me. There would be no one to sit with me or even to hold my hand. No one could step in and take the treatments for me. No stunt double would be hired to take the hard hits—no action to be accomplished by proxy. To have the radiation extinguish the cancer, I had to be there. The isolation made me acutely aware that no human could help me. In the pain of such profound aloneness, God revealed Himself to me in the most amazing

and loving way. The Master of the universe did not remove me from that room or decrease the number of treatments which, of course, would have been more in my comfort zone. No. Rather, I realized it was just Him and me, and He assured me that His presence was enough. His words in 2 Corinthians 12:9 became real to me (see verse below).

Here's the thing: we do not realize how far His grace reaches until we find ourselves in a circumstance we never thought we would be facing and one that, perhaps, we think is beyond His reach. Jesus has been my Savior for many years and, therefore, I have had a relationship with God the Father for many, many moons. But what I discovered was a completely new and wonderful level of a deeper connection with the Lord during a very dark time in my life.

Struggles in life have a funny way of turning one's perspective upside down. It was not that I did not know the truth about God's promises before—I did. I mean I loved the Lord and had given my heart to Him. I was learning about Him and growing closer to Him. However, through the trial of my cancer, His words became alive. No longer were they made up of mere ink on pages—they became an experience.

The Israelites were not so different than us today. When they were getting ready to cross the Jordan into the Promised Land, they knew they would face overwhelming dangers and fearful circumstances. Additionally, their leader Moses would not be going with them, but God assured them that He would be there with them (see Deuteronomy 31:6 below). He gives us the same promise.

So, this is not a testimony of how God healed me physically, although He did do exactly that. And I'm so thankful for His touch on me. While my body was healing, my victory of finding a true relationship with God was also taking place.

Circumstances change, diagnoses are handed out, treatment must be endured. But along with those things, we have the sweet and blessed assurance of His presence.

Be encouraged! God loves you so much. No matter what you are facing right now or what may come later, He will be right by your side all the way. Be encouraged, Tammy

Tuesday
Scripture: "But he said to me, 'My grace is sufficient for you, for my power is made perfect in weakness.' Therefore I will boast all the more gladly about my weaknesses, so that Christ's power may rest on me.'" (2 Corinthians 12:9)

Reflect, Activate: When have you felt very weak—physically or emotionally or spiritually? How does it help you to know God's power is there to help you when you feel weak? In other words, think of how it would be (or maybe was at some point for you) to not know of His power to help you in your weaknesses.

Wednesday
Scripture: "Be strong and courageous. Do not be afraid or terrified because of them, for the LORD your God goes with you; he will never leave you nor forsake you." (Deuteronomy 31:6)

Reflect, Activate: Look up other Scriptures telling us to not be afraid (there are many). Be honest about what you are afraid of and then pray and give those fears to God.

Thursday
Scripture: "And surely I am with you always, to the very end of the age." (Matthew 28:20)

Reflect, Activate: When have you felt the presence of Jesus more profoundly than usual? Was it during a difficult time or maybe a jubilant one?

Friday
Scripture: "You intended to harm me, but God intended it for good to accomplish what is now being done, the saving of many lives." (Genesis 50:20)

Reflect, Activate: When have you asked God, "Why?" Maybe it was about some event that did not seem fair or didn't make sense. But then later you looked back and saw God's plan in it. Remember—there are some things we will never understand this side of heaven, but we still can trust in a loving Father that He, indeed, has a plan.

Saturday and Sunday
Scripture: "And we know that in all things God works for the good of those who love him, who have been called according to his purpose." (Romans 8:28)

Reflect, Activate: Think of a particular blessing the Lord has given you. Then look at all the events and people leading up to that blessing and how He worked all of it together for your good.

Prayer for Week: Lord, some circumstances seem so painful and difficult at the time. When those happen, help me to remember Your goodness and that You are working out a higher purpose.

WEEK 28

Don't Miss the Call

> "The King will reply, 'I tell you the truth, whatever you did for one of the least of these brothers of mine, you did for me.'"
> (Matthew 25:40)

Don't miss God's call! What do I mean by that? Well, if we know that God is a trustworthy guide who knows everything about us and knows just where to take us, then can we trust He will make His voice known to us as well? When you cannot see anything, then you have to trust God as your guide to lead you to where He wants to use you.

God's Word says He will allow us to go through things in life so we can be there for others (see 2 Corinthians 1:3-5 below). He knows where we have been and what we have been through. God also knows exactly how He wants to use the experiences in our lives so we will be able to understand and meet the needs of the people we encounter. He places people in our path for us to lend a hand and open our hearts to. You see, I believe there are many opportunities in our lifetime, and He handpicks each one of us at an appointed time to reach out to specific person. Usually that person will be going through something we have experienced. If we had not been in that place already, we would not understand what that person is going through.

So, God may be calling you! Are you ready to answer the call? Let me elaborate with this example: I had a friend who struggled with cancer for quite some time. Why would God allow to her suffer for so long? Have you ever had a similar question? This friend felt she did not have a purpose and was just existing. I think her feelings of loneliness and not feeling needed were justified! But what she did not realize was that God was using her illness to reach the people who had been coming to help her. Because she was such a delight and such a positive witness through her pain, the people around her saw without a doubt Who was sustaining her. I think God specifically chose those people to minister to her needs so they could learn and grow and even be ministered to by her. It is possible those people had experienced something similar or were close to someone who had. Therefore, they would know how to be there for her, or it also could have been a learning experience for them. Either way, God had His reasons!

I believe God sometimes will keep us here on this earth even when, like my friend, we think there is no purpose at all. Remember—God sees the big picture. Even though it may feel like all we are doing is suffering, there are many hidden purposes. One that comes to mind in her situation is: if she had not been so sick and needy, she would not require help from others. Isn't it true that for us to have opportunities to serve, there has to be someone in need? There is nothing like being an answer to someone else's prayer. People need to be restored, and God wants to use us, His people, to do just that. Will we be the hands and feet of our Lord Jesus Christ, answering His call to reach out to people to make a difference? Remember, where God guides, He provides. Oh, the blessings God has waiting for us!

Now let's take a look at it from a different perspective, from the other side for a moment. God may have handpicked certain people in my friend's church or neighborhood to serve and comfort her, but who missed that call. Maybe they were distracted or overwhelmed with needs of their own, and her situation just did not quite get their attention. How sad when we let God's calling pass us by to be there for someone just because life consumes us. We can miss out on the blessings of serving others and being used mightily by God.

It is not always a time factor due to busyness that keeps us from serving others who are experiencing difficulties (like those who are sick or financially or spiritually needy, etc.). Perhaps people do not respond to the needs of others, not because they do not care, but because they just do not know how to respond at all. They may have feelings of helplessness, inadequacy, or they might just be overwhelmed by their own issues. So, what can you do? Seek the Lord, my friend, and just be yourself. Look for those opportunities to help those in need. You may have some reluctance for fear of feeling some of the other person's pain. Although it is possible you will feel sad because they are sad, it is not necessary to experience the full range of what they are going through. Just be yourself! A visit to a hurting person does not have to be lengthy or a regularly scheduled one; just give out of your heart. Reaching out could be as simple as sending a card or making a phone call.

It is amazing at how extending a hand to someone who is in distress can mean so much. They could be lonely, isolated, sick, grieving, or hungry; there are so many needs all around us. Think about how you would like to be treated if you were in their place. When a situation presents itself, prayerfully consider what God would have you to do. Ask Him for divine appointments, ones that only He can set up. If He orchestrates something, IT WILL NOT BE A BURDEN. Just be a willing vessel, and He will do the rest! Do not use your energy to do what only God can do. He will show you what your part is. Wait for God's plans to develop for you, and it will never be overwhelming. If you do feel yourself becoming overwhelmed, you may not be doing what God has called you to do. You can ask Him, "in light of my circumstances, God, what would You have me do?" God is the only one who knows exactly what each one of us can handle.

Understand this—human beings throughout all history have felt buried in the mire of their circumstances. Life can be so consuming at times! Likewise, people through the ages have needed one another. Some of us have more on our plates than we feel we can handle.

Along with natural abilities, God has also given us gifts to equip us as believers for the purpose of ministry. He expects us to use those abilities and gifts (see Romans 12:6 below). However, He does not use the unwilling, and He will not force any of us to serve Him. His part is to equip, empower, and prepare us for service. Our only part is to be faithful and available. You may already be reaching out to those in your workplace or neighborhood or at home with your children. We can minister to people anywhere at any time. You do not have to miss God's call! When you feel a longing to fill a need in someone else's life, listen to those thoughts. Pray and get involved, and you will be more blessed than you can imagine. God bless you all, as you seek His direction for your lives, Iris.

Tuesday
Scriptures: "We have different gifts, according to the grace given to each of us." (Romans 12:6a)

"It was he who gave some to be apostles, some to be prophets, some to be evangelists, and some to be pastors and teachers, to prepare God's people for works of service, so that the body of Christ may be built up until we all reach unity in the faith and in the knowledge of the Son of God and become mature, attaining to the whole measure of the fullness of Christ." (Ephesians 4:11-13)

Reflect, Activate: What do you feel your God-given gifts are? If you don't know, prayerfully ask Him to show you. Then when you know what the gifts are, ask Him how you can use them to serve others and glorify Him.

Wednesday
Scriptures: "He will always instruct you, and he will never leave you." (Psalm 32:8)

"Be still, and know that I am God; I will exalted among the nations, I will be exalted in the earth." (Psalms 46:10)

Reflect, Activate: What has God called you to do today? Tomorrow? Long-term? Remember, He will give you everything you need to accomplish anything He asks of you.

Thursday
Scriptures: "Two are better than one, because they have a good return for their work: If one falls down, his friend can help him up. But pity the man who falls and has no one to help him up!" (Ecclesiastes 4:9-10)

"Praise be to the God and Father of our Lord Jesus Christ, the Father of compassion and the God of all comfort, who comforts us in all our troubles, so that we can comfort those in any trouble with the comfort we ourselves have received from God. For just as the sufferings of Christ flow over into our lives, so also through Christ our comfort overflows." (2 Corinthians 1:3-5)

Reflect, Activate: Do you know someone who needs comfort or encouragement today? Consider making a phone call or sending a card or gift.

Friday
Scriptures: "Each man should give what he has decided in his heart to give, not reluctantly or under compulsion, for God loves a cheerful giver." (II Corinthians 9:7)

"Take my yoke upon you and learn from me, for I am gentle and humble in heart, and you will find rest for your souls." (Matthew 11:29)

Reflect, Activate: Pray and ask God what and who you can do something for. It may be something today or in the near future.

Saturday and Sunday
Scriptures: "And we know that in all things God works for the good of those who love him, who have been called according to his purpose." (Romans 8:28)

"Now to him who is able to do immeasurably more than all we ask or imagine, according to His power that is at work within us, to him be glory in the church and in Christ Jesus throughout all generations, for ever and ever! Amen." (Ephesians 3:20)

Reflect, Activate: What difficult circumstance have you experienced that later you looked back on and saw the good God brought out of it? If you are in one right now, trust the Lord to bring that good, even though you cannot see it.

Prayer for the Week: Lord, show me what gifts You have given me and how to use them for Your glory. Is there some act of kindness I can show to someone today or in the near future? Thank You that You never ask us to do anything without giving us the tools to make it happen.

WEEK 29

God Never Changes

"Your word, Lord, is eternal; it stands firm in the heavens." (Psalm 119:89)

My day at work was busy. I did not even take a lunch break. When I arrived home, my husband was getting food out of the refrigerator for dinner. I paused and looked at him, being all domestic and everything. I realized that life just isn't what it used to be. We are older. We may reside in the same bodies, but odd shiftings of sorts are taking place. A house once loud and busy with three boys is now quiet. The dynamic of the entire neighborhood has changed in the 25 plus years we have lived here. Many people have passed away, and new, younger owners live in the houses. Others, like us are empty nesters, and we are now approaching the ages of the neighbors we can considered the "older" people of the block when we first moved here.

Life consists of a series of changes we have to adjust to. Kids grow up and leave to do their own thing, jobs evolve, or we take new ones, and important people in our lives die. It can feel like we are on a perpetual merry-go-round, because we are a part of a fluid society and world. More than ever before, people travel to and even move to different states or countries. It is not unusual to have 12 to 15 jobs in a lifetime. Complete career changes, even as a person gets older, are not rare at all.

So, how do we survive and live well in an ever-shifting world? There is one we can count on to stay constant: God our Heavenly Father. We can be assured that no matter what is going on around us, no matter what unforeseen circumstance may arise, He does not change. His promises and what He says in the Bible has, and will always, remain the same.

When the Lord spoke through His prophet, Malachi, it was about the rebellion of the Israelites and how erratic they were in their loyalty to Him. The only thing they were consistent about was their inconsistency in their actions towards God. Sometimes they were obedient to God but most usually they disobeyed Him even though He always provided for them and remained faithful to His promises (see Malachi 3:6 below).

How amazing that we do not ever have to worry that God is going to change His promises or loyalty to us, His children. He is the steady force we can count on. As humans, it can be difficult to understand the concept of having someone we can lean on and completely trust. But God is not human (and we thank Him for that)—He is perfect. He sent His perfect Son to die for us and to be that "steady" we can always, without fail, turn to and depend on regardless of anything we encounter. He is not like sand that shifts as you step on it; He is a rock that cannot be moved. What comfort and assurance! Praise God and pass the blessings on! Tammy

Tuesday
Scripture: "Jesus Christ is the same yesterday and today and forever." (Hebrews 13:8)

Reflect, Activate: Some people are in our lives for only a season, but some are long-time friends and supporters. Think of all the people who have been a significant part of your life for a long time. Thank Jesus for both groups of people, but especially the long timers.

Wednesday
Scripture: "I the LORD do not change. So you, the descendants of Jacob, are not destroyed." (Malachi 3:6)

Reflect, Activate: Look up Scriptures that talk about the steadiness of the Lord. How does that attribute of God encourage you?

Thursday
Scripture: "The grass withers and the flowers fade, but the word of our God stands forever." (Isaiah 40:8, NLT)

Reflect, Activate: Many things are here today and gone tomorrow. God has given us many things of beauty to enjoy – what are some of those things for you?

Friday
Scripture: God is not human, that he should lie, not a human being, that he should change his mind. Does he speak and then not act? Does he promise and not fulfill? (Numbers 23:19)

Reflect, Activate: Think of some accounts in the Bible where people lied or betrayed or broke a promise. What were the consequences? Now, think about a time when you were on the receiving end of something similar. Isn't it comforting to know that God will never, ever do that to us?

Saturday and Sunday
Scripture: "Every good and perfect gift is from above, coming down from the Father of the heavenly lights, who does not change like shifting shadows." (James 1:17)

Reflect, Activate: Recall a time when you gave a someone what you considered to be "the perfect gift." However, it turned out the receiver was not as thrilled as you anticipated. Perhaps, it was not the right color or size or maybe they just did not like it. We cannot possibly know every detail about other people. Now consider how every gift from the Lord is perfect. He knows us intimately and knows exactly what we want and need. He can never give us the wrong gift.

Prayer for Week: Lord Jesus, thank You that You never change. Show me what "sand" I am trying to walk on and depend upon. Help me to turn my trust to You, my Rock. Amen and so be it!

WEEK 30

The Tale of Gunnar and Balto

"Jesus replied, 'What is impossible with men is possible with God.'"
(Luke 18:27)

One morning while listening to Song Time Radio, a Christian radio program out of Cape Cod, Massachusetts, I heard the inspiring story of Gunnar and Balto. It took place in January of 1925. A diphtheria epidemic threatened to wipe out the population of Nome, Alaska. An antidote serum was needed to arrest the epidemic and help people to get well. But there was a problem. The area was engulfed by horrendous snowstorms. The raging gusts of wind seemed suicidal to travel through by ground; air travel was impossible.

The people of Nome began to pray. Desperate SOS's were sent out. The only response was from some men 600 hundred miles away in Anchorage who had dog sled teams. These men knew the trip was nearly impossible, but they also knew that with God all things are possible. So, they answered the call, fully aware of the dangers to themselves and to their dogs. The distance itself made it no easy task.

Three dog sled teams set out in faith to step up to the challenge to save a village and its people. Knowing the people of Nome were praying for them inspired and encouraged these brave men. It seemed like every time they made progress, another snow squall would hit and nearly knock them over. Temperatures reached dangerous levels at 30 below and under. About half-way through the journey, two out of the three teams decided the trip was impossible. "If we continue, we will surely die of frostbite or be killed another way. We're turning back." The remaining team led by Gunnar and his lead dog, Balto, did not quit, however. Gunnar said, "Give me the serum, we're moving on. If the people of Nome do not get this antidote, the whole town will be lost."

"This is a suicide mission, you'll never make it," someone said. "My Master is calling," Gunnar replied.

So, Gunnar and Balto and the rest of the team pressed on. When Gunnar commanded, "Hup!" Balto would get up, no matter how cold or miserable the weather was. Balto obeyed his master and pressed on. In a similar manner, Gunnar also persevered and obeyed his Master's voice, our Lord. As the lone team moved on, the temperatures were so frigid that Gunnar could hardly move his hands. Ice stuck to his eyelashes, but he continued with God's grace.

With 60 miles to go, Gunnar was supposed to meet up with another dog sled team for the final leg of the trip. However, he could not find them and had to keep going. The fierce winds and snow squalls knocked the sled over and Gunnar broke his leg and several ribs. By this time, Balto had a frozen leg. Yet when Gunnar yelled, "Hup!" Balto obeyed his master and led the other dogs on into the storm. Finally, they reached their destination. The serum was distributed. A town and its people were saved, all because of the sacrifice and determination of a man and his dogs. What was behind this heroism? The power of prayer!

Months later, Gunnar had the privilege to testify at a press conference in New York of God's faithfulness during their trek to Nome. He also spoke of how his faith was strengthened because he knew the people of Nome, Alaska, were praying. Knowing that encouraged him to continue, even when it looked hopeless. Gunnar gave God, the prayers of the faithful saints of Nome, and his faithful dog, Balto, all the glory. In 1925 a statue of Balto standing alone was erected in New York City's Central Park. It gives tribute to Balto's heroism in pulling a sled through seemingly insurmountable circumstances and terrible weather conditions to save a town during that time.

Are you facing storms in life that are making it seem impossible to reach your destination? I want to encourage you, my friend, to pray. Also pray for others to reach their destinations and witness how great our God is. You see, more often than not, life will be challenging. It may seem that all the forces of nature are coming against you, just like what a man and his faithful dog faced so long ago in Alaska. You may think all of life is against you, leaving you frustrated as you get knocked over and broken. Maybe you feel as if all is lost. Press on, because the goal that God has set for you is well worth the struggle to get there. The storms will come—that is inevitable. Jesus even told us we would have trouble in this life. But as we look to Him, our Master, who is the author and finisher of our faith, the peace and rest and rewards that you need will come as you keep your eyes on Him.

One of my favorite accounts in the Bible is when Jesus told Peter to walk toward Him on the water. Peter was able to stay atop the water as long as he kept his eyes on the Lord. Then he lost that focus and looked to the storm around him and began to sink into the sea. Isn't that how this life can be? The storms will always be with us. But if we keep our eyes fixed on our Savior and walk toward Him, we will not be overtaken by the troubles that can seem to surround us.

As Balto and Gunnar did—obey the Master's voice, and reap the rewards in the end! Blessings, Iris

Tuesday
Scriptures "fixing our eyes on Jesus, the pioneer and perfecter of faith. For the joy set before him he endured the cross, scorning its shame, and sat down at the right hand of the throne of God." (Hebrews 12:2)

Reflect, Activate: Think of a time in your life that was so difficult that all you could do was to "fix" your eyes on Jesus. How did He help you in that situation? Think about someone who may need to be encouraged by your story of faith. Tell them!

Wednesday
Scripture: "I have told you all this so that you will have peace of heart and mind. Here on earth you will have many trials and sorrows; but cheer up, for I have overcome the world." (John 16:33, NLT)

Reflect, Activate: Looking back, what situations have you encountered that seemed desperate by the world's definition, but yet during them you had perfect peace? Remember those times next time you meet a difficult circumstance.

Thursday
Scripture: "'Lord, if it's you,' Peter replied, 'tell me to come to you on the water.' 'Come,' he said. Then Peter got down out of the boat, walked on the water and came toward Jesus. But when he saw the wind, he was afraid and, beginning to sink, cried out, 'Lord, save me!' Immediately Jesus reached out his hand and caught him. 'You of little faith,' he said, 'why did you doubt?' And when they climbed into the boat, the wind died down. Then those who were in the boat worshiped him, saying, 'Truly you are the Son of God.'" (Matthew 14:28-33)

Reflect, Activate: What is distracting you today? Think of it in the form of a storm like the disciples experienced on the Sea of Galilee that day. Then intentionally turn your mind and eyes toward the Lord and let Him draw to Himself and away from the distraction.

Friday
Scripture: "Call to Me, and I will answer you, and show you great and mighty things, which you do not know." (Jeremiah 33:3, NKJV)

Reflect, Activate: What great and mighty things have you seen God do in your life? Make a list and then thank Him!

Saturday and Sunday
Scripture: "Then you will call on me and come and pray to me, and I will listen to you. You will seek me and find me when you seek me with all your heart." (Jeremiah 29:12-13)

Reflect, Activate: Have you ever searched on the Internet or otherwise for someone or some information you need, but it seems as if what you are trying to find is hiding? What an amazing thing that we will always find God when we search for Him! He is not trying to hide from us – He wants us to find Him. Pray to Him today for something you need, and then watch Him work in the situation!

Prayer for the Week: Lord, thank You that we can always come to You knowing You hear us and that You will show us amazing things if we ask. Help me to keep my eyes fixed on You even when great troubles seem to be all around me.

WEEK 31

Around Life in 80 Years

"I have told you all this so that you will have peace of heart and mind. Here on earth you will have many trials and sorrows; but cheer up, for I have overcome the world." (John 16:33, NLT)

This life can be exciting, challenging, and devastating—sometimes all in the same day. Every single one of us has a story to tell about our own personal journey. Whether your life lasts 20 or 80 years, there are no two lives exactly alike. Every joy, every bump in the road, and all those people we encounter along the way have shaped us into who we are today. If we let

Him, God can take the good and bad things and mold us into who He wants us to be. We do not have to be at the mercy of the obstacles that try to deter us from the good in life.

God's Word says that whether you follow Jesus or not, things are going to happen that we will call unfair (see Matthew 5:45 below). Frankly, some circumstances and events we meet are not fair by any definition. What about the parents who lose a child to cancer? Or a spouse who leaves because they decide a younger person is more attractive? No one would say those things are fair. God's promise is not for the absence of trials and hard times. In fact, Jesus told his disciples just the opposite (see John 16:33 above).

The difference is this: if we know the Lord as our Savior, we are not alone when the challenges come. We can meet every hindrance on our journey with the confidence that He is there alongside of us. We are not without the help we need to get through anything we may come up against. Without God, the journey's bumps and potholes can be downright terrifying. But with the Lord, we do not have to be afraid. He constructed the whole highway, and He gives us the necessary vehicles and tools to navigate it successfully. We will even be able to help someone down the road going through what we have already experienced.

Yes, there will be many unfair things happen in life. The other side of it, though, is that the grace we receive from God is not fair either. We do not deserve it; there is nothing we can do to earn it. This is a gift from Him, and what a gift it is. Praise be to God that we do not get what we deserve for we would all be in trouble!

Turn to God. Let Him take the lead and show you the way. Ask Him to show you the path He has laid out just for you. Step by step He will guide you to an abundant life with heaven as the eternal destination. Praise the Lord! Isn't it exciting? In His Name and Love, Tammy

Tuesday
Scripture: "But I tell you, love your enemies and pray for those who persecute you, that you may be children of your Father in heaven. He causes his sun to rise on the evil and the good, and sends rain on the righteous and the unrighteous." (Matthew 5:44-45)

Reflect, Activate: Who have you watched go through a difficult time and came out on the other side with stronger faith and a powerful testimony of God's goodness? How did it boost your faith and bring you comfort?

Wednesday
Scripture: "Let us then approach God's throne of grace with confidence, so that we may receive mercy and find grace to help us in our time of need." (Hebrews 4:16)

Reflect, Activate: What need do you have today that can bring to the Lord in prayer? Ask Him for His help and guidance. He will not let you down. Have others pray if you feel you can tell them about the issue.

Thursday
Scripture: "Jesus answered, 'I am the way and the truth and the life. No one comes to the Father except through me.'" (John 14:6)

Reflect, Activate: This verse makes it very clear that Jesus is the one and only way to God the Father. Read all of chapter

14 and write down the verses that are especially meaningful to you today.

Friday
Scripture: "The thief comes only to steal and kill and destroy; I have come that they may have life, and have it to the full." (John 10:10)

Reflect, Activate: Think about how you can live your life in a more abundant way. Perhaps you need to take up that hobby you have ignored for years or maybe volunteer in an area of your church you've never served in before. What is God leading you to do right now in your life?

Saturday and Sunday
Scripture: "For it is by grace you have been saved, through faith—and this is not from yourselves, it is the gift of God—not by works, so that no one can boast. For we are God's handiwork, created in Christ Jesus to do good works, which God prepared in advance for us to do." (Ephesians 2:8-10)

Reflect, Activate: Look up other Scriptures talking about grace. What does His grace mean to you?

Prayer for Week: Lord Jesus, thank You for the abundant life you have given me. Thank You it is Your grace that saves me!

WEEK 32

In His Presence is Fullness of Joy

"You make known to me the path of life; you will fill me with joy in your presence, with eternal pleasures at your right hand." (Psalm 16:11)

These days we hear so much about depression, anxiety, mood swings, etc. Sleep deprivation is so prevalent in our society. Every time we turn the television or radio on, we hear how relief can be achieved with medications. The lack of peace and rest in our culture has really become quite alarming. Why is this? If we are living in a world that is full of God's glory, then why is there such a lack of peace?

God promises us His peace and rest. So why are so many of us living in anxiety and unrest? Granted, there may be nutritional and chemical reasons for this. We do live in an environment which is toxic, both chemically and stressinduced, but I believe there are also spiritual reasons for the lack of peace in our world today. I feel the reason some of us are struggling so much is because many people have no relationship at all with God. Did you know that in His presence is fullness of joy?

If we are not cheery and restful, our bodies cannot heal. In fact, we can become quite sick, even if we were not in a physically weakened condition to begin with. Lack of a relationship with God will, undoubtedly, cause a person to feel stressed out. A bumper sticker I've seen states this very simply: "Know Christ, Know Peace. No Christ, No Peace."

Where is the security in your future without God to turn to? May I boldly say that without God, we are nothing? Salvation not only gives us eternal life with God, it also brings us into a personal relationship with Him. God says that He has given us eternal life, not just in heaven, but here, too.

You see, healing and peace and rest—even laughter—are byproducts of a personal relationship with God. On our own, we will not have any of these qualities for long if we are lucky enough to have them at all. They will not be found in things or staying busy. True lasting peace and joy can only be consistently present as we live a life in a relationship with Jesus Christ, the author and perfecter of our faith.

If you struggle with fear, consider this: A relationship with God will, literally, stop fear. God's voice tells you a different story than what you see with your natural eyes. While experiencing trouble, there is nothing better than God's grace. Yes, things will happen to us, but isn't it comforting to know that the voice of truth says to not be afraid? God bless you as you seek Him and rest in Him. Moving forward in His steps, Iris

Tuesday
Scriptures: "A man's spirit sustains him in sickness, but a crushed spirit who can bear?" (Proverbs 18:14) says: "A cheerful heart is good medicine, but a crushed spirit dries up the bones." (Proverbs 17:22)

Reflect, Activate: What circumstance in your life now or in the past has felt crushing? Ask God to make your heart cheerful again – He is faithful to do so.

Wednesday
Scripture: "Come to me, all you who are weary and burdened, and I will give you rest. Take my yoke upon you and learn from me, for I am gentle and humble in heart, and you will find rest for your souls. For my yoke is easy and my burden is light." (Matthew 11:28-30)

Reflect, Activate: Give God all that burdens you today! What do you think the yoke of Jesus is?

Thursday
Scripture: "And anyone who believes in God's Son has eternal life. Anyone who doesn't obey the Son will never experience eternal life but remains under God's angry judgment." (John 3:3, 6 NLT)

Reflect, Activate: Look up other Scriptures that talk about obedience. Is there an area in your life where you feel God urging you to become more obedient?

Friday
Scripture: "The thief comes only to steal and kill and destroy; I have come that they may have life, and have it to the full." (John 10:10)

"Peace I leave with you; my peace I give you. I do not give to you as the world gives. Do not let your hearts be troubled and do not be afraid." (John 14:27)

Reflect, Activate: Find other Scripture pertaining to the peace Jesus brings us. Write them down and read them whenever you feel your peace being threatened.

Saturday and Sunday

Scripture: "Let us fix our eyes on Jesus, the author and perfecter of our faith, who for the joy set before him endured the cross, scorning its shame, and sat down at the right hand of the throne of God." (Hebrews 12:2)

Reflect, Activate: What do you think it means to "fix our eyes on Jesus"?

Prayer for Week: Lord, help me to give all that I feel burdened with over to You so that I may have peace in my heart and life.

WEEK 33

God's Presence in the Dark Pit

"Where can I go from Your Spirit? Or where can I flee from Your presence? If I ascend into heaven, You *are* there; if I make my bed in hell, behold, You are there." (Psalm 139:7-8, NKJV)

Corrie ten Boom and her sister, Betsie, spent time in the Nazi concentration camps during World War II. They experienced a truly dark pit. Betsie died in the camp, but Corrie survived. She lived out the rest of her life traveling around the world telling people how God's presence was there, even while living in what seemed like hell on earth.

In *The Hiding Place*, Corrie relates her experiences of being imprisoned by the Nazi's during World War II. She and her family were arrested for hiding Jews in their house in Holland.

Reading this book every few years points out any selfishness or whining that might have crept into my being.

God has promised that He will not leave us. No matter what your dark pit of despair is right at this moment, God is with you. He will not abandon you. In fact, He can use anything, including something as horrific as a Nazi concentration camp, to bring about good. We can find joy, just as Corrie and Betsie did, during the darkest times in our lives.

True joy does not come from how we look, what we have, or what our circumstances are. Pure and complete joy comes only in God's wonderful presence. I believe He desires to surround us in His glorious presence so that we might find peace in this life. The God of the universe is right beside us, and there is nothing better or more comforting. He is there in our most wonderful times full of light and in our worst and darkest days.

No matter what is going on, if we are followers of the Lord of lords then we are His witnesses. We can be good witnesses, or we can be bad witnesses. What is inside us will show on the outside. How much better and how much more glory it brings to God if we let His love and joy show on our countenance. There is nothing more beautiful than seeing a Christian's face radiate with God's light. Don't you just love seeing someone who is full of the love of Christ? If someone notices that joy in us, they will be uplifted and encouraged. So, ask Him and allow Him to cleanse you from within and then fill you with His joy so that it will project from you onto others. In other words, choose to let God's joy shine through you!

What dark pit of despair is threatening to steal your joy right now? Take your situation and all your hurts to Jesus and lay them at His feet. Then rest in His care and His joy will return to you. His love for you and me is bigger and deeper and stronger than anything this life can throw at us. If His presence and joy could be felt in a Nazi concentration camp, then I believe He has the same for us now, right where each of us is. In His love and hope, Tammy

Tuesday
Scripture: "Let your conduct be without covetousness; be content with such things as you have. For He Himself has said, 'I will never leave you nor forsake you.'" (Hebrews 13:5, NKJV)

Reflect, Activate: How does envying what someone else has make you unhappy? How can you be more content with what you have?

Wednesday
Scripture: "If God is for us, who can ever be against us?" (Romans 8:31b, NLT)

Reflect, Activate: Think about what this verse is saying. We don't ever have to worry about someone who is against us. All we need is God on our side, and He is. How was He on Moses' side when he was confronting Pharoah? How was He on Joseph's side when his brothers sold him to the Egyptians?

Thursday
Scripture: "A happy heart makes the face cheerful, but heartache crushes the spirit." (Proverbs 15:13)

Reflect, Activate: Can you remember a time when you truly felt as if your heart was broken? How did the Lord bring joy back into your heart and therefore bring healing?

Friday
Scripture: "Cast your cares on the LORD and he will sustain you; he will never let the righteous be shaken." (Psalm 55:22)

Reflect, Activate: What burden(s) do you need "cast upon the Lord" today? Go to Him and pray about them.

Saturday and Sunday
Scripture: "And the God of all grace, who called you to His eternal glory in Christ, after you have suffered a little while, will himself restore you and make you strong, firm and steadfast." (1 Peter 5:10)

Reflect, Activate: How has God brought you out of a place of suffering and re-established you? If you are in a place of suffering right now, lean on this passage and promise.

Prayer for Week: Praise You, God, for Your amazing love and for all Your comforting promises. Be glorified in my life and help me to shine Your light into the darkness of the world.

WEEK 34

Have You Ever Felt Like a Target?

"In you, LORD, I have taken refuge; let me never be put to shame. In your righteousness, rescue me and deliver me; turn your ear to me and save me. Be my rock of refuge, to which I can always go; give the command to save me, for you are my rock and my fortress. Deliver me, my God, from the hand of the wicked, from the grasp of those who are evil and cruel. For you have been my hope, Sovereign LORD, my confidence since my youth. From birth I have relied on you; you brought me forth from my mother's womb. I will ever praise you." (Psalms 71:1-6)

The first four verses of Psalm 71 deal with problems. But then an interesting thing happens. It goes from voicing problems and petitions, to crying out to God in praise. David, the author, beseeches God in verse 4 to deliver him from evil and cruel men. He is telling God that he feels as if he has a bull's-eye on his back, allowing the enemy to get a clear shot. Then David begins to praise God in faith, thanking Him for His help and deliverance. By placing his hope and confidence in God, David has the assurance that God will be faithful to deliver him again, as He always has. In verse 6, David declares, "From birth I have relied on You."

David may have felt like a sitting duck, but he knew he had to leave the battle to the Lord. When he began to sing praises to his heavenly Father, the Lord set ambushes against the adversary. This enemy was left defeated. David knew that eventually there would be rest on every side, just as there was for King Jehoshaphat in 2 Chronicles (see below).

Have you ever felt like you had a literal bull's-eye painted on your back? You see, I do not believe you have a target on your back. I think life and circumstances happen. We are in this world and are subject to its problems. Turn your gaze toward heaven and see the deliverance God has for you. Praise Him, for He is holy, just, and faithful! You can trust Him. Thank God that He is there with your provision waiting as your turn your fears and concerns over to Him.

Sometimes God uses pain to protect us, and sometimes He uses pain to redirect us. You can trust that God is always there when the storms of life come. I believe He allows them so we will look to Him. There is no pain so intense or storm so violent that God's hope cannot overcome.

So together, let's sing the song that states: "Holy is the Lord God almighty; the earth is full of His glory." God is right beside you. He is ready to help you—all you have to do is ask. So, the next time you feel like a living target, choose praise instead of problem listing! Lift up a heart of exaltation to God. Praise Him and be ready for what happens. You may be surprised by the change that takes place in the atmosphere all around you. Your own outlook in your circumstances may even change. Sing to Jesus who is the King of kings and the Lord of lords. One of the greatest comforts God gives us is that He has a plan for each one of us. Pray and discover the design He has for your life. Remember, He is all you need. Moving forward in His steps, Iris

Tuesday

Scripture: "I have told you these things, so that in me you may have peace. In this world you will have trouble. But take heart! I have overcome the world." (John 16:33)

Reflect, Activate: Jesus does not promise us a life without troubles. However, He does promise we can have peace in spite of troubles. How does it encourage you to know Jesus has already overcome the world?

Wednesday

Scripture: "But seek first His kingdom and His righteousness, and all these things will be given to you as well." (Matthew 6:33)

Reflect, Activate: What does it mean to "first seek His kingdom and His righteousness" in a day-to-day, practical way?

Thursday

Scripture: "But as for me, I will always have hope, I will praise You more and more." (Psalm 71:14)

Reflect, Activate: Search out other Psalms that are about praising God. How does offering up praise to God bring you hope?

Friday

Scripture: "Do not be afraid or discouraged because of this vast army. For the battle is not yours, but God's. As they began to sing and praise, the LORD set ambushes against the men of Ammon and Moab and Mount Seir who were invading Judah, and they were defeated. And the kingdom of Jehoshaphat was at peace, for his God had given him rest on every side." (2 Chronicles 20:15, 22, 30)

Reflect, Activate: Is there a "battle" you find yourself in today? Give it over to God and then rest in Him to take care of it.

Saturday and Sunday
Scripture: "And they are calling to one another, 'Holy, holy, holy is the LORD Almighty; the whole earth is full of His glory.'" (Isaiah 6:3)

Reflect, Activate: We can praise God with our words in prayer or by singing worship songs or by our actions. Think about some of your favorite songs you sing as praise to Him. What are some "action" ways you can praise Him, such as encouraging a friend, taking a meal to someone, etc.

Prayer for Week: Lord, help me to know how to praise You, and thank You for being willing and able to take on my battles.

WEEK 35

Not Alone

"Keep your lives free from the love of money and be content with what you have, because God has said, 'Never will I leave you; never will I forsake you.' So we say with confidence, 'The Lord is my helper; I will not be afraid. What can mere mortals do to me?'" (Hebrews 13:5-6)

When do you feel the most alone? Is it in the middle of the night when you awake to a quiet house and troubling thoughts race through your mind? It may be when you feel like the whole world cannot possibly understand what you are going through, and you feel unloved. Let's face it, sometimes it does feel like we are all alone. This usually happens when we are going through some stressful situation such as a divorce or an illness or death of a loved one.

There are a couple of truths we need to grab a hold of here: First, we are never alone—not really. God has promised He will never leave us or forsake us. Sometimes we need to have the presence of the Lord "with skin on"—someone right here, in the flesh, to support us and be by our side through a trial. It is my experience that God always provides that person or persons when we need someone to be His hands and feet.

Second, we do have to realize it is true that others cannot possibly fully know how we feel in a particular situation. The variables in each trial for every individual are so vast. Think about it: we are all in different states of mind, and where we are spiritually is never the same. Also, family dynamics, job situations, relationships, etc., all come into play with numerous possible differences. For example, if someone loses a parent to death, that person is going to react completely different from anyone else.

However, God uses people to come alongside us when we are going through difficulties. Sometimes all we need them to say is, "I'm here for you." They do not have to understand completely or know exactly how we feel. In the same way, when we see others going through struggles, we can come alongside them by just loving them. That can mean physically giving them a hug or praying with them. Perhaps even something like picking up some groceries for them or taking them for a drive. There is something painful and beautiful about weeping when others weep and laughing when they laugh. Doesn't God want us to encourage people the way we would want to be encouraged?

God did not design us to live this life isolated and alone. He made us for fellowship with each other and with Him. He wants us to come to Him with our concerns and problems. Remember—He is there, even if you do not feel Him. When we cry out to Him in our need or when we reach out to another in his/her need, we are fellowshipping with the Lord. We are walking closely with Him.

The desire of my heart is to walk so closely with the Lord that when He calls me home, it will not be a long journey. How can we accomplish that? By praying, reading, and meditating on His Word; listening for His voice; and reaching out to others like Jesus did when He was on this earth.

So, if you are feeling alone right now, ask God to help you to trust Him for all your needs. Just pray, "I know You are here with me, Lord, even though I may not feel or see You all the time." Be ready to reach out to others when they are hurting. Take heart, for He is faithful to never leave you, and He always knows what is best for you. In His love and comfort, Tammy

Tuesday

Scripture: "Praise be to the God and Father of our Lord Jesus Christ, the Father of compassion and the God of all comfort, who comforts us in all our troubles, so that we can comfort those in any trouble with the comfort we ourselves receive from God." (2 Corinthians 1:3-4)

Reflect, Activate: Do you know of someone who needs comfort or encouragement right now? Maybe they are going through something similar to one of your past experiences. Reach out to them.

Wednesday

Scripture: "Rejoice with those who rejoice; mourn with those who mourn." (Romans 12:15)

Reflect, Activate: Is there someone who is rejoicing over an answered prayer or a joyous occasion? Let them know you are rejoicing with them and are happy for them. Or lend a shoulder or ear to someone who needs to cry about something.

Thursday
Scripture: "The LORD God said, 'It is not good for the man to be alone. I will make a helper suitable for him.'" (Genesis 2:18)

Reflect, Activate: We are not meant to do life alone. Think about all the people in your life, past and present, whom God has given you. Think about (and/or write down) what each of those people brought to your life. Then maybe contact one or more and tell them what they mean to you.

Friday
Scripture: "No one will be able to stand against you all the days of your life. As I was with Moses, so I will be with you; I will never leave you nor forsake you." (Joshua 1:5)

Reflect, Activate: When did you feel like you were heading into a land of unknown (like Joshua) and needed God to go with you?

Saturday and Sunday
Scripture: "let us draw near to God with a sincere heart and with the full assurance that faith brings, having our hearts sprinkled to cleanse us from a guilty conscience and having our bodies washed with pure water. Let us hold unswervingly to the hope we profess, for he who promised is faithful. And let us consider how we may spur one another on toward love and good deeds, not giving up meeting together, as some are in the habit of doing, but encouraging one another—and all the more as you see the Day approaching." (Hebrews 10:22-25)

Reflect, Activate: Who do you know who needs encouragement today? Go and encourage them in the Lord with a call or message, etc. If you cannot think of anyone, ask Jesus to show you someone in need, even if it is the worker at the grocery store or a homeless person on the corner.

Prayer for Week: When I feel alone, Lord, bring to my remembrance Your promise of never leaving or forsaking me. Help me to recognize when You are calling me to comfort someone who feels alone and afraid.

WEEK 36

Are We Responsible for the Truth?

"If anyone, then, knows the good they ought to do and doesn't do it, it is sin for them." (James 4:17)

At one time, all of us were in darkness and not responsible for the truth. But once we know the truth, we become responsible for it. In other words, let's say you never learned that stealing was bad. You might be tempted to do it, possibly not fully understanding the consequences. However, once you learn stealing is not right, you become responsible to fulfill the law of truth. You see, when we know right from wrong and do wrong anyway, God holds us more accountable. The consequences for wrongdoing may be greater. This is because God entrusted you with a responsibility and you ignored it.

All of this was reinforced to me when I was watching an old movie about Bonnie Parker and Clyde Barrow. Some of you may remember that they were the Farmer's Bank Robbers from the 1930s. After meeting in January 1930, Bonnie and Clyde were companions for approximately four years as they carried out their crime spree together that ended in their violent deaths. They went down in history as blood thirsty killers. But what if things had been different for them? What if they had come to know the Lord instead? How did they start life anyway?

Bonnie was an honor roll student in high school where she excelled in creative writing. Her father was a bricklayer and was an interim pastor at a local church. Clyde's life started out differently. He was born in Texas just south of Dallas to a poor farming family. His first arrest in 1926 was when he was just in his teens. He cracked safes, robbed stores, stole cars, and then went on to bigger things like robbing banks. He was never taught right from wrong.

Clyde's goal in life was not to gain fame and fortune from bank robberies. Rather, he hungered for revenge against the Texas prison system for the abuses he suffered while serving time for earlier crimes. What an aspiration! We do not know for sure if Clyde was offered the prayer of salvation or not. But what if he had been? Would he have gone down the same road? I'm not so sure! What happened when he died? Did God hold him accountable for his actions?

Bonnie, I believe, was held more accountable because, according to history, she heard the Word and was taught right from wrong. Allegedly, she grew up hearing the Gospel in her home. When she met Clyde, who really did not know any different, she could have shared the Gospel and what she knew about right and wrong. Instead, she was more attracted to all the excitement, and she chose to follow Clyde down a dead-end road to destruction. They were shot more than 50 times in an ambush. What greater consequences can someone suffer for doing wrong than to be gunned down in such a brutal way?

Are there lessons to be learned from history? I think so! That is why the stories in the Bible are there. God wants us to learn from people in the Bible, from their victories, their mistakes, and various situations. His Word is like a compass for us to know how to live and what direction to go. Will you follow the Lord's leading in the Truth and end your life with victory, or will you follow another voice and end your life in tragedy? Maybe not like Bonnie and Clyde, but my friends, tragedy for some can mean not knowing God and spending eternity apart from Him. What will your choice be? Rejoicing in the Truth, Iris

Tuesday
Scripture: "The whole Bible was given to us by inspiration from God and is useful to teach us what is true and to make us realize what is wrong in our lives; it straightens us out and helps us do what is right." (2 Timothy 3:16, NLT)

Reflect, Activate: What are some verses that have been particularly "teaching" for you in your life? For example, maybe Matthew 7:1, "Do not judge, or you too will be judged."

Wednesday
Scripture: "To the Jews who had believed him, Jesus said, 'If you hold to my teaching, you are really my disciples. Then you will know the truth, and the truth will set you free.'" (John 8:31-32)

Reflect, Activate: Look up the definition of disciple. How does knowing God's truth set one free?

Thursday
Scripture: "For rulers hold no terror for those who do right, but for those who do wrong. Do you want to be free from fear of the one in authority? Then do what is right and he will commend you. For he is God's servant to do you good. But if you do wrong, be afraid, for he does not bear the sword for nothing. He is God's servant, an agent of wrath to bring punishment on the wrongdoer." (Romans 13:3-4)

Reflect, Activate: How does your behavior differ now than before you became a Christ follower?

Friday
Scripture: "It would have been better for them not to have known the way of righteousness, than to have known it and then to turn their backs on the sacred command that was passed on to them." (2 Peter 2:21)

Reflect, Activate: If Bonnie (from Bonnie and Clyde) grew up knowing the gospel, why do you think she chose to take up with someone like Clyde? What can we learn from this piece of history?

Saturday and Sunday
Scripture: "If I had not come and spoken to them, they would not be guilty of sin; but now they have no excuse for their sin." (John 15:22)

Reflect, Activate: Read all of John, chapter 15. Write down the verses that especially speak to you.

Prayer for Week: Lord, bring to my mind Your instructions as I go through each day. Thank You for those commandments, there for my protection.

WEEK 37

Being Ready

"While they were stoning him, Stephen prayed, 'Lord Jesus, receive my spirit.' Then he fell on his knees and cried out, 'Lord, do not hold this sin against them.' When he had said this, he fell asleep." (Acts 7:59-60)

Stephen was killed because he refused to deny Jesus. He had peace as he was dying, even though stoning must be a horrible way to die. I cannot help but wonder what I would do in that same circumstance. If I was given a choice of dying a painful, slow death or simply saying, "No" to my Savior, what would I choose? As a Christian, the appropriate answer would be, "Well, of course I wouldn't deny Jesus as my Lord." But that is easy to say when you are not standing alone, surrounded by people waiting to throw rocks at you to end your life. You cannot get away and saving yourself is out of the question. All you have to do to avoid this horrific way to die is to say, "Jesus? I don't know Him."

The Bible promises us that no matter what we go through here on this earth, it will all be worth it. I am convinced the paradise waiting for us in heaven is so much better than we can possibly imagine in our limited human minds. So, what is death then? Is it something to be feared? No, not when you have accepted Jesus as your Savior. We can be assured that He will bring us through whatever we meet to be with Him for all eternity. What comfort this brings to me! I know God will give me the grace and peace to bear whatever comes my way, even death.

How do we prepare ourselves to face whatever life brings? I am convinced it was no accident that Stephen had enough strength to face his accusers and stay obedient to God in his final moments. I think he had built his relationship with the Lord over time. Then when he was confronted with a life-or-death choice, he could easily make that decision without hesitation or regret. He knew God was with him. He knew his murderers could kill his physical body, but they could not take his soul.

We build a solid relationship with our heavenly Father by communicating with Him; that is, praying to Him and getting to know Him through reading and meditating on His Word. We fellowship with other believers to gain strength. Remember, God is always with you no matter what may happen in your life. He loves you and wants you to have His peace and presence, just as Stephen did, even when staring death in the face.

Ask for His help in your circumstances, and He will be there for you. Stay close to Him, Tammy

Tuesday
Scripture: "I consider that our present sufferings are not worth comparing with the glory that will be revealed in us." (Romans 8:18)

Reflect, Activate: Think of your "paradise" vacation spot on this earth. Is it sitting on a beach with the sound of ocean waves nearby? Or is it a cabin up in the mountains with breathtaking views? I believe our heavenly home will be as amazing as we can imagine in our heads and then a thousand times beyond that.

Wednesday
Scripture: "The Lord will rescue me from every evil attack and will bring me safely to his heavenly kingdom. To him be glory for ever and ever. Amen." (2 Timothy 4:18)

Reflect, Activate: Try to have an eternal perspective on your day. Whatever struggle you are facing today, remember this is not all there is.

Thursday
Scripture: "But he said to me, 'My grace is sufficient for you, for my power is made perfect in weakness.' Therefore I will boast all the more gladly about my weaknesses, so that Christ's power may rest on me." (2 Corinthians 12:9)

Reflect, Activate: There are many theories about what the "thorn in the flesh" Paul talks about ahead of this verse. Many think it was a physical problem or maybe depression. Whatever it was, he knew Christ's power was sufficient for him to endure it. What do you feel like is you "thorn in the flesh"?

Friday
Scripture: "Dear friends, don't be afraid of those who want to kill your body; they cannot do any more to you after that." (Luke 12:4, NLT)

Reflect, Activate: Next time you feel afraid, remember this verse. Look up other Scripture telling us to not be afraid. If you are prone to fear or anxiety, make a list of verses that comfort you in this area. Read them whenever you need to dispel fear.

Saturday and Sunday
Scriptures: "Be joyful always; pray continually; give thanks in all circumstances, for this is God's will for you in Christ Jesus." (1 Thessalonians 5:16-18)

"Your word is a lamp to my feet and a light to my path." (Psalm 119:105, NKJV)

"Let us hold tightly without wavering to the hope we affirm, for God can be trusted to keep his promise. Let us think of ways to motivate one another to acts of love and good works. And let us not neglect our meeting together, as some people do, but encourage one another, especially now that the day of his return is drawing near." (Hebrews 10:23-25, NLT)

Reflect, Activate: What does it mean to pray continually? For what should you give thanks to God today? How has God's Word been a light to your path?

Prayer for Week: Lord Jesus, help me to be ready for whatever each day brings. Bring your peace upon me and all of my loved ones, family and friends, as they meet different challenges.

WEEK 38

God Is Always Listening

"The Lord will hear when I call to him." (Psalm 4:3b)

In the silence of the night when your household lies resting, do unsettling thoughts sometimes dominate your mind? Perhaps you have been careful not to voice your concerns with others because you did not want to worry them or did not think they would understand. But in a desolate moment you feel all alone with your struggles. You wish you could share them with someone and that they would comfort you.

I have good news—God hears you! He is with you with His ear always bent toward you, waiting for you to invite Him into your situation. You do not have to continue feeling alone. The closer we get to the Lord, the less we will feel alone. Call out to the Lord and tell Him your concerns. Let Him comfort you; He is always ready to listen.

The Bible tells us of a man, named Enoch, who walked very closely with God. He was one of only two men (the other was Elijah-see 2 Kings, chapter 2) in the Bible who did not die but who God "took" because he was in close fellowship with God. By that I mean that Enoch went with God to heaven into eternity because his spiritual walk with God was so intimate.

Can we learn a lesson from Enoch? I would have to say an emphatic, "Yes!" As believers, no matter how hard our journey is or where it leads us, our relationship with God will last through eternity. Without God in our lives—not knowing Jesus Christ as our personal Savior—our path here can be just that, time on earth and then nothing. Friends, God created us for fellowship. In the Bible, God tells us about His love for us and the benefits of walking closely with Him.

Walking closely with God is an act of obedience to Him. In Deuteronomy (see chapter 28, verses 1-14), God talks about the blessings of obedience. Then from verse 15 to the end of the chapter, you will read about the curses of disobedience. So, let me ask you this, friends: In a day and age where life can seem so uncertain and you need a solid anchor to hold you through the challenges you face, whom today will you serve? None of us can serve two masters. Remember, there are many false prophets out there ready to steal the limelight from God and threaten to control you, leading you down a dangerous path.

I cannot emphasize enough how loving our God is. The God who created you loves you. All He expects is that you be faithful to Him and call Him Father. He does not require you to give up freedom or things that are fun; He wants and expects you to enjoy the life He has given you. If you live your life according to His Word, you will have true joy and peace and a freedom from Him with lasting contentment. He loves you, so will you give Him the love and honor He deserves? Try it and see what happens. You will never hunger or thirst again.

Know that you are loved; know there are treasures beyond measure waiting for you in His presence. God bless you as you love on Him today and expect great and mighty things, especially while experiencing trials. He does not promise a life without problems, but He does promise His presence during them. He will not leave you; He will provide all you need. Rejoicing in the Truth, Iris

Tuesday
Scriptures: "After the birth of Methuselah, Enoch lived in close fellowship with God for another 300 years, and he had other sons and daughters. Enoch lived 365 years, walking in close fellowship with God. Then one day he disappeared, because God took him." (Genesis 5:22-24. NLT)

"By faith Enoch was taken from this life, so that he did not experience death; he could not be found, because God had taken him away. For before he was taken, he was commended as one who pleased God." (Hebrews 11:5)

Reflect, Activate: What does it mean to you to live in close fellowship with God? What areas in your relationship with Him do you feel you can work on to become closer to Him?

Wednesday
Scriptures: "I have told you these things, so that in me you may have peace. In this world you will have trouble. But take heart! I have overcome the world." (John 16:33)

Reflect, Activate: Yes, there is much trouble in the world. Do you believe we can have true peace during our troubles? When have you experienced that?

Thursday
Scripture: "I Myself said, 'How gladly would I treat you like sons and give you a desirable land, the most beautiful inheritance of any nation. I thought you would call me Father and not turn away from following me.'" (Jeremiah 3:19)

"And my God will meet all your needs according to the riches of his glory in Christ Jesus." (Philippians 4:19)

Reflect, Activate: We are to be God's hands and feet at times. Is there someone you know for whom you could help supply a need?

Friday
Scripture: "This is a sacred day before our Lord. Don't be dejected and sad, for the joy of the Lord is your strength!" (Nehemiah 8:10b, NLT)

Reflect, Activate: When you feel the Lord's joy do you feel stronger? What other verses can you find that speak of the joy we can have in Him?

Saturday and Sunday
Scripture: "...but whoever drinks the water I give them will never thirst. Indeed, the water I give them will become in them a spring of water welling up to eternal life." (John 4:14)

Reflect, Activate: What do you think Jesus is referring to as the water He gives?

Prayer for Week: Lord, teach me how to be in close fellowship with You and with other believers. Thank You for always hearing when I pray and providing for my every need.

WEEK 39

He's in the Boat

"A furious squall came up, and the waves broke over the boat, so that it was nearly swamped. Jesus was in the stern, sleeping on a cushion. The disciples woke him and said to him, 'Teacher, don't you care if we drown?' He got up, rebuked the wind and said to the waves, 'Quiet! Be still!' Then the wind died down and it was completely calm." (Mark 4:37-39)

"Jesus is in the boat with you"—a comment, Paul, one of my pastors, made few years ago on the above Scripture reference in one of his sermons. I have thought about it many times since then. How wonderful to know that no matter what "boat" or storm we find ourselves in, Jesus is on board with us. Amen and so be it—He is right here with me.

The storm Jesus calmed that day on the Sea of Galilee was real, and it was dangerous. The Sea is situated between hills that are 2,000 feet high with cool, dry air on one side and semi-tropical, warm, moist air on the other sides. It sits at 680 feet below sea level. This causes large temperature and pressure changes, which can result in sudden, violent storms. Being a shallow, small body of water, it is more easily whipped up by the wind of a storm more than a deeper, bigger lake. The waves the disciples were experiencing were bashing the boat so violently the men were afraid they were going to die. And there was Jesus, asleep. How could He be relaxed enough to take a snooze when they were on deck, working and fighting to stay alive?

We all have "storms" in our lives—those times when we really think we are not going to survive. I'm not necessarily talking about only in a physical way. The tempest could be financial or relationship issues, a health crisis, or trouble at work or school. Troubling waves of life will come regardless of who you are, how much money you have, or how old you are. But we can have peace within while the storms of life rage on around us.

My grandmother had five children by the time she was 23 years old. I asked her one day if there were days she thought she wasn't going to "make it." She didn't hesitate to say, "Of course. Many times!"

We have not been promised an easy life. If someone says that you will never experience any trials, you can be assured they are telling you large and fictional tale. However, Jesus did promise He would be with us in all the tribulations we meet and go through. When the waves come, even when they threaten to capsize our boat—He is there to bring us peace. All you or I have to do is ask Him to be with us. Be encouraged! Tammy

Tuesday

Scripture: "Keep your lives free from the love of money and be content with what you have, because God has said, 'Never will I leave you; never will I forsake you.'" (Hebrews 13:5)

Reflect, Activate: Think about a specific time that, looking back, you can see now how Jesus was by your side. Perhaps at the time, you did not realize that He was the one who calmed your storm.

Wednesday

Scripture: "When you pass through the waters, I will be with you; and when you pass through the rivers, they will not sweep over you. When you walk through the fire, you will not be burned; the flames will not set you ablaze." (Isaiah 43:2)

Reflect, Activate: How does the assurance of this verse comfort you? What do "the waters" and "the rivers" represent to you?

Thursday

Scripture: "Have I not commanded you? Be strong and courageous. Do not be afraid; do not be discouraged, for the LORD your God will be with you wherever you go." (Joshua 1:9)

Reflect, Activate: Knowing God is always with us is a comfort as a Christian. But how may it be an uncomfortable thing if you were not a follower of Christ? When have you seen the difference this makes in someone's life, such as facing a death of a loved one as a Christian versus as a non-Christian?

Friday

Scripture: "I will not leave you as orphans; I will come to you." (John 14:18)

Reflect, Activate: An orphan is defined as a child who has lost both parents to death. These children cannot fend for themselves and need help in every area to survive. Now think of the above verse and replace the word "orphan" with what it means: "I will not leave you to fend for yourselves"—etc.

Saturday and Sunday
Scripture: "The LORD himself goes before you and will be with you; he will never leave you nor forsake you. Do not be afraid; do not be discouraged." (Deuteronomy 31:8)

Reflect, Activate: What does it mean to you to know the Lord is walking ahead of you? How does that help you to not be afraid or discouraged?

Prayer for Week: What a comfort to know You are always with us, Jesus! No matter the circumstances, I know You are right by my side to see me through.

WEEK 40
Dealing With Difficult People

"But to you who are listening I say: Love your enemies, do good to those who hate you, bless those who curse you, pray for those who mistreat you. (Luke 6:27-28)

"Bless those who persecute you; bless and do not curse. (Romans 12:14)

Everyone has dealt with difficult people at one time or another—who, no matter what you do, are right and you are wrong. We can never live up to what they demand of us, whether it be physically, emotionally, or spiritually. Manipulation can become a well-used tool as they strive to get what they want. I'm talking about when we've tried to help someone or to make the relationship with that person better, and they still don't come around or respond to the truth. You may have tried everything you can think of, and they still choose to live in disharmony and, perhaps, play the role of the victim. Whatever the situation, God expects us to pray for and bless them. We are to love demanding and self-centered people. However, we do not have to take their problems upon ourselves, nor do we have to take abuse from them. We also do not want to become like them. In other words, we need to be careful in being around them so that we do not take on some of their ungodly characteristics.

We know Jesus encountered difficult people and situations (think of the Pharisees), and He knew we would, too. I think that at some point, after perhaps many incidents of being bombarded with emotional darts, God will guide us to shake the dust from our feet and move on.

In the late 1950s, James Vicary of New Jersey brought the notion to everyone's minds that theaters were splicing scenes of food into movies to suggest hunger and thirst on unsuspecting movie watchers. He claimed that these subliminal messages spoke to people's subconscious and boosted sales at the concession stands. Even though this was proved to be an urban legend, Mr. Vicary planted the thought into Americans' minds that they could easily be manipulated into doing things they would not do otherwise. Manipulation is a favorite tool of the enemy.

So, where does our part come in? How do we protect ourselves from being manipulated and from being in relationships involving difficult people? Obviously, we cannot avoid all contact with people who are hard to get along with. However, as much as we can, we need to guard ourselves from being in situations that may cause us to be exposed to the wrong kind of influences. For example, if you are looking for a godly husband, should you cruise the bars every night hoping to meet Mr. Right? The enemy can very quickly sneak in with the temptation, "Don't you want a little of this? Don't you desire that? A little won't hurt." However, if you give into these seemingly harmless enticements, the enemy now has a foothold in your life; you have opened the door to him. And yes, it often does lead to bigger and more dangerous sins and mindsets. That is how, I believe, people end up turning away from the Lord.

The Lord wants us to fill our thoughts with the things of God and walk away from evil influences. Like Jesus, we are to protect our minds so that we do not fall into the enemy's trap. Guard your heart, my friend. Be a light where you can be. However, there may be times you sense someone you are trying to minister to is becoming manipulative and wanting only what he/she wants for selfish gain. If that happens, take the advice of God's Word to shake the dust off your feet and move on before you are dragged into a situation you were never meant to be in. Remember how easily you can be devoured by traps the enemy sets before you. The key is to know the truth of what God is saying to you by staying in His Word and praying continually. Stay close to Him and you will not be deceived by the lies of the enemy. Watch what you read, what you see on television, and who your closest friends are. Be careful to not allow the enemy to slowly draw you down a road you never intended to be on, toward temptations and destruction. Do not be one of his victims by giving into what the world says is pleasing. Jesus offers something much better. Rejoicing in the Truth, Iris

Tuesday
Scriptures: "Finally, brothers and sisters, whatever is true, whatever is noble, whatever is right, whatever is pure, whatever is lovely, whatever is admirable—if anything is excellent or praiseworthy—think about such things." (Philippians 4:8)

Reflect, Activate: Take each of the words in the above Scripture (true, noble, etc.) and write down one thing it describes. For example, what does it mean to you that something is true?

Wednesday
Scripture: "Whenever you enter a house, stay there until you leave that town. And if any place will not welcome you or listen to you, shake the dust off your feet when you leave, as a testimony against them." (Mark 6:10-11)

Reflect, Activate: Have you ever walked into a room or situation and felt unwelcome? How did it feel when you left that place?

Thursday
Scripture: "You will keep in perfect peace all who trust in You, all whose thoughts are fixed on you." (Isaiah 26:3, NLT)

Reflect, Activate: What is "perfect peace" to you? Today, intentionally turn your thoughts to God frequently and see how it affects your mood and overall day.

Friday
Scripture: "Don't waste what is holy on people who are unholy. Don't throw your pearls to pigs! They will trample the pearls, then turn and attack you." (Matthew 7:6, NLT)

"Do not be misled: 'Bad company corrupts good character.'" (I Corinthians 15:33)

Reflect, Activate: Think of an example of when someone (you or someone else) was led astray by the wrong people. Now, think of the people in your life who have led you in the right direction. Consider writing or calling them to thank them.

Saturday and Sunday
Scripture: "This is what the Sovereign Lord says: On that day thoughts will come into your mind and you will devise an evil scheme.'" (Ezekiel 38:10)

"The thief comes only to steal and kill and destroy; I have come that they may have life, and have it to the full." (John 10:10)

Reflect, Activate: The thief mentioned above is the opposite of Jesus. How has Jesus helped you live your life to the fullest?

Prayer for Week: Lord help me to guard my heart and mind against the enemy and all of his ploys to manipulate me. So, when someone is trying to lead me down the wrong path away from You, open my eyes to see that and then turn away.

WEEK 41

Going Around in Circles

"Be still, and know that I am God! I will be honored by every nation. I will be honored throughout the world." (Psalm 46:10)

A few years ago, a friend and I would take early morning walks during the week before I went to work. Every morning, I dragged myself out of bed at 5:30. Once I was able to prop my eyes open for more than a few seconds, I called Linda. Now this is tricky because my vision is blurry, and I have more than one "Linda" in my phone. It would not have been good to wake the wrong person up at that hour. By 6 a.m. we started our three-mile walk around the park and watched the day come to life. To aid in our fitness, we both bought "shape-up" shoes. I think they were supposed to work your legs more. Their soles are rounded (kind of in a boat shape) and thicker than other shoes, making you stand one-half inch or so taller. If you stood still, you kind of teeter-tottered, which was a little unnerving at first. One morning, Linda was getting ready when I arrived. But there was a problem: she had on one shape-up shoe and one regular shoe. We laughed, picturing me leaving her behind as I trucked on down the sidewalk—talking to myself—while she remained on one spot going around in circles. She would have been totally unbalanced and, eventually, dizzy.

As funny as that visual was in our minds, isn't it true of life? If we get out of balance, if we are spending too much time in one or two areas of our lives and ignoring the rest, everything may begin to spin out of control. It is much easier to maintain a healthy balance than to get back to that equilibrium from a place of teeter-tottering. Think of gymnasts: if they are not balanced on the apparatus they are performing on, it does not take much for them to topple over. They will lose points and possibly be completely out of the competition or worse, get injured. Everyday life is the same. When challenges come to us, we will be more equipped to handle them appropriately if we are standing steady.

Jesus wants to help us to find that stability—a way to organize our lives in the healthiest way possible. So, what do we do to get back into the right balance and what do we do if we find ourselves completely disjointed and out of whack?

First of all, stop and still your mind before the Lord (see Psalm 46:10 below). The New American Standard version says to cease striving. This is one of the hardest, most important things to do when you are feeling overwhelmed and unbalanced. It may feel like you are trying to stop a tsunami heading for your little hut on the beach. It is very hard to hear His "voice" through the noise of our busyness. Even Jesus took time to leave all the crowds and noise to be by Himself so He could pray. Second, ask Him to help you figure out what your next step is, how to prioritize your responsibilities, and what to hold onto and what to let go. He is faithful and will help you. Look and listen for His answer in His Word and when praying about it. Or the answer may come in words in a song or in the counsel of a good friend or pastor. It may even come to you as you sleep at night.

In our humanity, we sometimes develop this horrible diseased attitude that if someone asks us to do something seemingly good, we are obligated do it. Especially, if it is for church or for other people. If we say yes to everything, eventually we will become burned out, irritable, and guilt-ridden. In the end, it really is just a form of pride and martyrdom—we think we are the only ones who can "do the job right."

So, if you find yourself feeling out of balance or overwhelmed—pray to God that He will show you how to get back to where He wants you to be. He will help you to live a balanced life (and get the right shoes on) that will be fulfilling and an honor to Him and to those around you. In Him, Tammy

Tuesday
Scripture: "But Jesus often withdrew to lonely places and prayed." (Luke 5:16)

Reflect, Activate: Spend some "alone" time with the Lord in prayer and reading His Word. Pour your heart out and then listen for what He has to say.

Wednesday
Scripture: "LORD, hear my prayer, listen to my cry for mercy; in your faithfulness and righteousness come to my relief." (Psalm 143:1)

Reflect, Activate: Find other verses in the Psalms about crying out to God. David did it quite often. What is your favorite Psalm?

Thursday
Scripture: "I will bless the LORD who guides me; even at night my heart instructs me." (Psalm 16:7, NLT)

Reflect, Activate: Search out other Scriptures about God's guidance and instructions.

Friday
Scripture: "The thief comes only to steal and kill and destroy; I have come that they may have life, and have it to the full." (John 10:10)

Reflect, Activate: How are you living your life "abundantly"? Think about areas where, maybe, you want and need to live it more abundantly.

Saturday and Sunday
Scripture: "Come to Me, all you who labor and are heavy laden, and I will give you rest. Take My yoke upon you and learn from Me, for I am gentle and lowly in heart, and you will find rest for your souls. For My yoke is easy and My burden is light." (Matthew 11:28-30, NKJV)

Reflect, Activate: What do you think it means to take Jesus's yoke upon yourself? Maybe research this verse and what others think it means.

Prayer for Week: Thank You, Lord, that we can always come to You for rest for our weariness. Help me not to let the busyness of this life cause me to miss what You have for me.

WEEK 42

We Do Have a Purpose

"You made all the delicate, inner parts of my body and knit me together in my mother's womb. Thank you for making me so wonderfully complex! Your workmanship is marvelous—how well I know it. You watched me as I was being formed in utter seclusion, as I was woven together in the dark of the womb." (Psalm 139:13-15, NLT)

Consider this: God created you and has called you by your name. Not only that, but He actually has a job description that fits perfectly with who you are. If your heavenly Father were to advertise a job that only you could fill, what description would it contain? What qualifications would God ask for that you are specifically gifted in? Look at it from the opposite standpoint. What would you desire in applying for a position with Him?

Let me elaborate from my own experience. A few years ago, I went through months of arduous testing in search of an answer to a perplexing medical issue. Five spots found on a brain MRI confirmed what the doctors already knew about the disease I have. A CT scan was ordered to further determine if another spot seen on my spine was cancer or not. When I met with the doctor after the scan, he declared that I did not have cancer. Needless to say, all the medical personnel involved were very surprised, and my family and friends were elated. I sent out an e-mail to friends explaining my doctor's findings and sharing how faithful God was with His presence and peace as I dealt with this. Many people stood faithfully with me in prayer during this time and responded with words of encouragement. Here is an excerpt from one e-mail I received from a precious woman in my church:

> "Thank you for sharing yet another praise report about God's love and faithfulness. It is all for the glory of God! The Lord has made an amazing person named Iris whom He is pleased to use, and your inspiration and encouragement to us is priceless. What a job description—must love Me, must have a good sense of humor, and must be willing to be sick and go wherever I send her. Thanks again, Iris. Love, Pat"

I had never thought about how God has a specific "occupation" for each of us until Pat brought it to my attention. I was so grateful for the praise report from the hospital and then for that powerful and uplifting word from her. She told me that, although I have a lot of physical difficulties (part of my job specification), it is the very job He has ordained for me. He had me apply for a unique calling stemming from the personal experiences He allowed me to go through. Why? So that I can be there for others when they encounter similar life situations. Experiencing the difficulties and hardships in life helps us to appreciate the blessings that God gives us. To be truly empathetic toward others, it is necessary to have personally walked through some adversities. Remember that everything you encounter in life God can, and will, use to draw you closer to Him.

What about you? Are all your experiences—the trials, difficulties, and times of testing—giving you a lifetime of knowledge and skills so you can work for Him according to what He has for you to do? Are you using all of that to reach out and help others in similar trials that you've already navigated through and overcome?

Here's something else to ponder: If everyone decided to use their gifts and reach out according to what they can do, even if that is a little bit, what kind of world would we have? How would our churches be different? Would there be any needs left to meet?

So, think about the job description God has for you. Are you living it out? Are you working the assignment of your calling well? Consider writing out a summary like Pat did for me and look at the good all your hard labor will produce as you work for Him. God has a plan for your life. Seek Him in prayer by asking Him what that is specifically for you. He will guide you and direct you toward a fulfilling job for His kingdom. Blessings to you. Be loved today! Iris

Tuesday

Scripture: "I will give you hidden treasures, riches stored in secret places, so that you may know that I am the LORD, the God of Israel, who summons you by name." (Isaiah 45:3, NLT)

Reflect, Activate: What are some of the "treasures" God has given you? Think about talents you have, friends and family in your life, etc. Tell someone today what a treasure they are or have been to you.

Wednesday

Scripture: "For just as each of us has one body with many members, and these members do not all have the same function, so in Christ we, though many, form one body, and each member belongs to all the others. We have different gifts, according to the grace given to each of us. If your gift is prophesying, then prophesy in accordance with your faith; if it is serving, then serve; if it is teaching, then teach; if it is to encourage, then give encouragement; if it is giving, then give generously; if it is to lead, do it diligently; if it is to show mercy, do it cheerfully." (Romans 12:4-8)

Reflect, Activate: List each of the gifts in the verses above and then write what you think they mean or synonyms of the words. What are your gifts from God?

Thursday
Scripture: "Praise be to the God and Father of our Lord Jesus Christ, the Father of compassion and the God of all comfort, who comforts us in all our troubles, so that we can comfort those in any trouble with the comfort we ourselves receive from God." (2 Corinthians 1:3-4)

Reflect, Activate: What "affliction" have you experienced that allowed you later on to help someone who was going through a similar situation? Or did someone help you through a difficulty they had already experienced?

Friday
Scripture: "Do not judge, or you too will be judged." (Matthew 7:1)

Reflect, Activate: Is there something or someone you are being judgmental towards? Ask God to show you and then ask Him to help you not have that judgmental attitude.

Saturday and Sunday
Scripture: "Give, and it will be given to you. A good measure, pressed down, shaken together and running over, will be poured into your lap. For with the measure you use, it will be measured to you." (Luke 6:38)

Reflect, Activate: What do you think first two sentences of the verse mean? Remember—you cannot out-give God! What can you give today? It doesn't have to be money; it can be your time or talents. Maybe even to call or visit someone who needs encouraging.

Prayer for Week: Lord I open my heart and mind for the "job" that you have for me to do to further Your Kingdom here on this earth. May I be aware of opportunities you set before me that will lead into Your calling on my life.

WEEK 43

Jailbreak

"About midnight Paul and Silas were praying and singing hymns to God, and the other prisoners were listening to them. Suddenly there was such a violent earthquake that the foundations of the prison were shaken. At once all the prison doors flew open, and everyone's chains came loose. The jailer woke up, and when he saw the prison doors open, he drew his sword and was about to kill himself because he thought the prisoners had escaped. But Paul shouted, 'Don't harm yourself! We are all here!' The jailer called for lights, rushed in and fell trembling before Paul and Silas. He then brought them out and asked, 'Sirs, what must I do to be saved?' They replied, 'Believe in the Lord Jesus, and you will be saved—you and your household.'" (Acts 16:25-31)

Paul and Silas were thrown in jail in Philippi and put into stockades for preaching the gospel. The jailer was commanded to guard them carefully. I wonder what the other inmates thought about the two men. Perhaps at first they thought the two preachers were crazy. But after listening to their joyful singing, I'm guessing those in nearby cells probably wanted to know where Paul and Silas found such joy in the dire circumstances of prison. How could they be praise God while being incarcerated? When he thought the prisoners had all escaped, the jailer knew he would be the one blamed for their breakout. He thought his only choice was to kill himself.

However, all of the prisoners were still there! The jailor recognized the power of God and that Paul and Silas' praising of their Lord and Savior had set them free from their physical bonds. I think he also understood they were free on the inside, too, and he wanted what they had. If you are beaten and thrown into jail for preaching the gospel of God and then can sing praises to that very same God, there must be something powerful and true about this Savior. Not only did He supernaturally open the physical doors of the jail, He also gave Paul and Silas peace even before those doors sprung open to free them.

Not all jails have walls and bars. What "prison" do you find yourself in? It could be an addiction or something in your past that continues to haunt you. Maybe it is health issues, a difficult relationship, or a trying job situation. Know this: God is there to give you joy and peace in any situation you are struggling with. If others see us rejoicing in the middle of difficulties and heartaches, they will find hope for their own situations. It could bring them to ask about this God we serve. Like the jailor in Philippi, our trials could be what draws them to the Lord and His saving grace. There is nothing, absolutely nothing He cannot see you through. Hallelujah and amen! Blessings, Tammy

Tuesday

Scripture: "Through Jesus, therefore, let us continually offer to God a sacrifice of praise—the fruit of lips that openly profess his name." (Hebrews 13:15)

Reflect, Activate: Read through and find Psalms (there are several) that are a praise to God. Then offer up your praise to Him for what He has done for you. You might even want to write a list of your blessings.

Wednesday

Scripture: "Rejoice in the Lord always. I will say it again: Rejoice! Let your gentleness be evident to all. The Lord is near. Do not be anxious about anything, but in every situation, by prayer and petition, with thanksgiving, present your requests to God. And the peace of God, which transcends all understanding, will guard your hearts and your minds in Christ Jesus." (Philippians 4:4-7)

Reflect, Activate: What does it mean to "let your gentle spirit be known to all people"? What are you anxious about today? Pray and give it over to God and watch His peace come in.

Thursday

Scripture: "Yet in all these things we are more than conquerors through Him who loved us. For I am persuaded that neither death nor life, nor angels nor principalities nor powers, nor things present nor things to come, nor height nor depth, nor any other created thing, shall be able to separate us from the love of God which is in Christ Jesus our Lord." (Romans 8:37-39, NKJV)

Reflect, Activate: How does it comfort you that there is absolutely nothing that can separate you from God and His love? Let someone know today that they are loved by God and by you!

Friday
Scripture: "Rejoice always, pray continually, give thanks in all circumstances; for this is God's will for you in Christ Jesus. (1 Thessalonians 5:16-18)

Reflect, Activate: How can you rejoice and give God thanks in your current circumstances? Do you know someone in a difficult situation who could use some encouragement today?

Saturday and Sunday
Scripture: "Even though the fig trees are all destroyed, and there is neither blossom left nor fruit; though the olive crops all fail, and the fields lie barren; even if the flocks die in the fields and the cattle barns are empty, yet I will rejoice in the Lord; I will be happy in the God of my salvation. The Lord God is my strength; he will give me the speed of a deer and bring me safely over the mountains." (Habakkuk 3:17-19, NLT)

Reflect, Activate: Think of instances when you knew, without a doubt, the Lord was your strength to get you through? What do you think the verse means that God will "give me the speed of a deer and bring me safely over the mountains"?

Prayer for Week: Lord, when I find myself in difficult circumstances, help me to be more prone to rejoicing than to complaining and whining. I know in my head that You make all things work together for good—help me to get that in my heart.

WEEK 44

Mayberry vs. Heaven

"I am leaving you with a gift—peace of mind and heart. And the peace I give is a gift the world cannot give. So don't be troubled or afraid." (John 14:27, NLT)

In September 2010, fans of *The Andy Griffith Show* came from all over the world to Mt. Airy, North Carolina, to celebrate the 50th anniversary of the first show's airing. Mt. Airy is widely thought to be the town the show was modeled after. As I read the article on this event, I was stirred by the enthusiasm of the people who enjoyed memories of the "good ole' days" and the simplicity of that time. They were remembering days when it was not the norm for a sheriff to carry a gun, unlike the world today. What a blessing it must have been to revisit a sitcom that had "so much love." This quote is from Andy Griffith himself, who from what I understand, had Christian values. I believe this show was based on biblical principles.

The Andy Griffith Show first aired on October 3, 1960, running for eight seasons. The final episode showed on April 1, 1968. This sitcom had 249 episodes, 159 of which were produced in black and white. By the sixth season, they began filming in color. The show depicted a simpler time; a time when neighbors sat on front porches and shared a cup of coffee or a soda pop. People actually spoke to each other in person. Email and texting, which I feel takes away from a personal connection, did not exist. Meeting with someone face-to-face, you can look that person in the eye and see an encouraging smile or feel a hug of assurance. Growing up, my neighborhood was similar to Mayberry in that everyone looked out for each other. I have many fond memories of being on our front porch or lawn and eating ice cream or drinking soda with people who lived on our street. What a sense of safety I felt from having this community around me during my childhood.

Whether you are old enough to remember watching it during its original seasons or you have watched syndicated reruns, *The Andy Griffith Show* causes us to relate to an uncomplicated life. The theme of show depicted the attitude of caring for one another, a perspective that seems to be more the exception than the rule now. These values lined up with what God's Word says as it instructs us how to live the life we were destined to live. (See Ecclesiastes 4:9-12 below.) We think about Aunt Bee's down-home cooking and Andy's closeness to the townspeople. Andy was more like a friend or family member to Mayberry's citizens and less like a sheriff. He had a special relationship with Barney, his deputy and friend from childhood. He was a caring father who struggled to raise his only son, Opie, after his wife's death. Andy taught him love and integrity, not by giving him things but with good old-fashioned discipline. His loving correction did not harm Opie but, in fact, made him stronger, more caring about others, and less self-seeking. Andy showed his son how to make decisions while also accepting the consequences of wrong choices.

Mayberry reminds me of another place and person—Heaven and our Savior, Jesus Christ. Andy was Mayberry's hero. Jesus is our hero while we are still on this earth dealing with our daily struggles. He is our way to heaven. We can lean on Him every step of the way to find victory, peace, assurance, and the love we all long for.

So, when people ponder and long for the "good ole' days," what are they actually longing for? I believe what we really yearn for is a relationship with God, whether we realize it or not. We are desperate to be in that place of security forever where there are no more tears or pain but only joy, happiness, and eternal peace. That, my friends, is Heaven—our real home! Mayberry's portrayal of such a safe and secure place gives us a glimpse of what we really long for. The warm feeling we experience when watching this classic sitcom is only a mere glimmer of what we have waiting for us in Heaven. The fact is that neither Mayberry nor this world is our real home.

If you find yourself hungering for that place of wonderful security, God can help you prepare for Heaven while you are still here on earth. Please see the prayer of salvation on page 3 of the book. Remember that God loves you and wants you to have the peace He offers to everyone who calls on His name. He longs for you come to Him just as you are so that He can help you become everything you yearn to be. In His love, Iris

Tuesday
Scripture: "Jesus answered, 'I am the way and the truth and the life. No one comes to the Father except through me.'" (John 14:6)

Reflect, Activate: What does Jesus mean by each of the three things He says in this verse? What about claims that there are multiple ways to heaven?

Wednesday
Scripture: "For to me, to live is Christ and to die is gain." (Philippians 1:21)

Reflect, Activate: What does it mean by: "to live is Christ"? What do you we gain when we die and leave this world?

Thursday
Scripture: "As Jesus was walking beside the Sea of Galilee, he saw two brothers, Simon called Peter and his brother Andrew. They were casting a net into the lake, for they were fishermen. "Come, follow me," Jesus said, "and I will send you out to fish for people." At once they left their nets and followed him." (Matthew 4:18-20)

Reflect, Activate: What do you think Peter's and Andrew's thoughts were when Jesus asked them to follow Him? Put yourself in their shoes—remember we know the end of the story, but then didn't.

Friday
Scripture: "Come to me, all you who are weary and burdened, and I will give you rest." (Matthew 11:28)

Reflect, Activate: What burden are you carrying today that you would like to give to Jesus? He is ready, willing, and able to carry it for you!

Saturday and Sunday
Scripture: "Two are better than one, because they have a good return for their labor: If either of them falls down, one can help the other up. But pity anyone who falls and has no one to help them up. Also, if two lie down together, they will keep warm. But how can one keep warm alone? Though one may be overpowered, two can defend themselves. A cord of three strands is not quickly broken." (Ecclesiastes 4:9-12)

Reflect, Activate: What relationship have you had or have, in which you felt like you held each other up at times? Can you think of someone who could use some "help getting up" right now?

Prayer for Week: Lord Thank for Your assurance of Heaven and the rest we will have when we get there. Thank You also that we can have that peace while still on this earth, no matter what is going on in the world.

WEEK 45

Get Moving

"Brothers and sisters, I do not consider myself yet to have taken hold of it. But one thing I do: Forgetting what is behind and straining toward what is ahead, I press on toward the goal to win the prize for which God has called me heavenward in Christ Jesus." (Philippians 3:13-14)

"Today," my friend said as we had lunch one day, "I give up on my New Year's resolutions. I tried as hard as I could, and all I accomplished was failure. I messed up last year and now this year is already a disaster." The date she declared it over? January 4.

Do you ever feel this way? That you might as well not even set goals? I do, and I'm sure everyone does at one time or another. I do think God wants us to formulate objectives and then reach for them. A new year can be a perfect time to lay out plans for what we want to make happen, but this can be done at any time. We do not have to wait for a January 1. Instead of establishing my own goals, as a follower of Christ, I need to pray and ask Him to help me know, write down, and then accomplish, the plan He has for me. Putting my intentions down on paper is important—that way I have a tangible reminder. It is also a good idea to find an accountability partner, someone you can share your goals and then your progress with.

Starting off with a clean slate is refreshing and energizing. I think taking time to reflect back on the past can be helpful. This is not to beat ourselves up with regrets, but to evaluate what we want to accomplish from here on out. I can take an honest look at areas where I failed and need to improve on, knowing God will forgive me if I ask Him and will also help me to learn and do better with those things today and in the future.

Such hope we have when we have the Lord! Every day, not just January 1st, is a new start with Jesus, our Savior. His faithfulness is great. That is not to say we should just write off what happened in days gone by with an attitude of carelessness. Look back but do not stay there. It is extremely important to not park ourselves in the past. We can have the assurance that when we do mess up (as we will in our humanness), God is ready and willing to allow us start over. He does not want us to live in our past regrets but to grow from them. Then the next time a similar circumstance comes up, we can apply what we learned and make things better.

So, ask yourself: what have I learned in the past year (or months or days) and how can I apply that knowledge to now?

What have I gotten away from that I need to get back to? How about making a bucket list? Then get moving! Go forward in what God wants you to do. Be encouraged because He has great things ahead for you. Tammy

Tuesday
Scripture: "Yet this I call to mind and therefore I have hope: Because of the LORD's great love we are not consumed, for his compassions never fail. They are new every morning; great is your faithfulness." (Lamentations 3:21-23)

Reflect, Activate: God gives us a fresh start every morning! Who, in your life, do you need to afford that same privilege to? Perhaps someone you need to forgive, including yourself.

Wednesday
Scripture: "Therefore, if anyone is in Christ, he is a new creation; old things have passed away; behold, all things have become new." (2 Corinthians 5:17, NKJV)

Reflect, Activate: How does your life after becoming a Christ follower differ from before? What areas are you still working on?

Thursday
Scripture: "Therefore, I urge you, brothers and sisters, in view of God's mercy, to offer your bodies as a living sacrifice, holy and pleasing to God—this is your true and proper worship. ² Do not conform to the pattern of this world, but be transformed by the renewing of your mind. Then you will be able to test and approve what God's will is—his good, pleasing and perfect will." (Romans 12:1-2)

Reflect, Activate: What does it mean to not be conformed to this world? Do you feel there are areas in your life that, perhaps, you have been conforming to but need to get back on track for God?

Friday
Scripture: "'For I know the plans I have for you,' declares the Lord, 'plans to prosper you and not to harm you, plans to give you hope and a future.'" (Jeremiah 29:11)

Reflect, Activate: How does knowing God wants to give each of us a hope and future bring you comfort and encouragement? Is there someone you know who needs to hear this today? Tell them!

Saturday and Sunday
Scripture: "Then I will give them one heart, and I will put a new spirit within them, and take the stony heart out of their flesh, and give them a heart of flesh, that they may walk in My statutes and keep My judgments and do them; and they shall be My people, and I will be their God." (Ezekiel 11:19-20, NKJV)

Reflect, Activate: God changes people's hearts, and then their actions should follow. Have you witnessed a person before and after they gave their heart to Jesus? How were they different? How did seeing their transformation help increase or renew your faith?

Prayer for Week: Dear Lord, help me to know what goals you want me to reach out for and then give me the ability and strength to accomplish them. Thank You that You never ask us to do something without giving us the necessary tools to do so.

WEEK 46

No Whining Please!

"...give thanks in all circumstances; for this is God's will for you in Christ Jesus." (1 Thessalonians 5:18)

During the Thanksgiving season one year, I realized my habit of complaining was being exposed for what it is—ugly. Believe me, I did not like what I saw when I started looking at myself to see what was really going on within. I still struggle with this habit, one that is way too easy to master and hang on to. Here are some of the ridiculous things I have grumbled about in the past, probably some even recently:

1) A driver pulls out in front of me and then drives—how dare he—five miles per hour below the speed limit.
2) A day turns cloudy and windy when I planned to take a walk, and now I must stay inside.
3) A new recipe fails for—how embarrassing—Thanksgiving dinner.
4) For the 5th time in a day, the radio station plays that song I am sick of. I know it talks about God, but let's put it to rest for a while.

Seeing the "whines" in print make me feel silly. Really? Are any of them that important in the scheme of eternity? Believe me, the above list is not conclusive, not even close. How dare I complain about such trivial stuff when I have so much to be thankful for! God has given me so much, not just materially, but in every other way, too.

Please understand—I am not minimizing the difficult issues of life or the incredible burdens some people carry on a day-to-day basis. Some people certainly have circumstances and issues worthy of being sorrowful over. No one makes this journey without experiencing times of darkness and confusion. Sometimes bad things happen to us or to our loved ones. It can be a challenge when you are in the middle of difficulties to find anything to be grateful for. Sometimes, we may have to hunt long and hard for them, but I am convinced there is always something to be thankful for.

The Apostle Paul was familiar with hardships, including imprisonment and beatings. He wrote about being thankful no matter what was going on. (See 1 Thessalonians 5:18 below.) That verse used to cause me pain and maybe even some anger. How could God expect us to always be thankful? What about a person who has dealt with chronic illness for many years? Or a parent who loses a child? There are overwhelming issues in life that look completely hopeless. Then I realized the verse says *in* all circumstances—not *for*. God knows when you are going through a rough stretch. He will help you get to the other side of whatever situation you find yourself in. You have a Savior who experienced all kinds of heartache and pain while on this earth. He knows your pain and suffering, and you are never, ever alone.

So, if you are going through a stormy time right now, try looking for things to be thankful for in your life. Ask God to show you what those things are and make a list. You may be surprised with what you come up with, and how you can still be at peace in the middle of some tough days. God loves you so much! He wants the very best for you. Be encouraged, Tammy

Tuesday
Scripture: "These sufferings of ours are for your benefit. And the more of you who are won to Christ, the more there are to thank him for his great kindness, and the more the Lord is glorified. That is why we never give up. Though our bodies are dying, our inner strength in the Lord is growing every day." (2 Corinthians 4:15-16, NLT)

Reflect, Activate: What difficulty are you experiencing now, and what can you find to be thankful about while in it?

Wednesday
Scripture: "Therefore, since we are surrounded by such a great cloud of witnesses, let us throw off everything that hinders and the sin that so easily entangles. And let us run with perseverance the race marked out for us, fixing our eyes on Jesus, the pioneer and perfecter of faith. For the joy set before him he endured the cross, scorning its shame, and sat down at the right hand of the throne of God. Consider him who endured such opposition from sinners, so that you will not grow weary and lose heart." (Hebrews 12:1-3)

Reflect, Activate: Everyone has experienced hostility from another person at some time. How does this verse help you when you think about some hostility you've dealt with?

Thursday
Scripture: "Don't worry about anything; instead, pray about everything; tell God your needs, and don't forget to thank him for his answers." (Philippian 4:6, NLT)

Reflect, Activate: What needs do you have today that you need to tell God about?

Friday
Scripture: "For we do not have a high priest who is unable to empathize with our weaknesses, but we have one who has been tempted in every way, just as we are—yet he did not sin." (Hebrews 4:15)

Reflect, Activate: How and when do you think Jesus was tempted? Read some of those accounts; for example, in Matthew 4.

Saturday and Sunday
Scripture: "And whatever you do, whether in word or deed, do it all in the name of the Lord Jesus, giving thanks to God the Father through him." (Colossian 3:17)

Reflect, Activate: Some things we do throughout our days can seem mundane. Try focusing on each task you do today as doing it for the Lord. Then look back later and see how your attitude was different because of that.

Prayer for Week: Lord, forgive me when I lose sight of how many blessings you have given. Help me to remember that You understand all the temptations and difficulties I meet.

WEEK 47

Balanced Living—God's Way

"As a chair needs four legs to be balanced, so we need God's Word to balance us so we don't fall over."~~Iris Smith/Tammy Maseberg

"But seek first his kingdom and his righteousness, and all these things will be given to you as well. Therefore do not worry about tomorrow, for tomorrow will worry about itself. Each day has enough trouble of its own." (Matthew 6:33-34)

I like the way the paraphrase version, The Message, puts it in Romans 12:11: "Don't burn out; keep yourself fueled and aflame."

What holds us up so we can live a balanced life? If we do not have some sort of equilibrium in our lives, we will eventually fall. While working and taking care of our families, we also need to incorporate rest, time with God, volunteer work and helping others, and recreation. Then there are our relationships which require time and energy. And of course, we need to take care of our health by exercising and eating right. With all those things to juggle, it is easy to wear ourselves out by running in too many directions all at once. So how can we find appropriate balance in this hectic and, sometimes, unpredictable world and live peaceful and productive lives?

I believe if we take time to pray to God at the beginning of each day that we will find rest, direction, and balance for that day. Jesus gave the perfect example to follow: This will help us to not "fall off the world," so to speak, as it spins crazily around us.

So, prayer and God's Word are the means to get to know Him better and better. We learn to trust him as He guides us in how to live—what to do and not do each day. We can have the assurance that no matter what happens, it will be okay. Then we will have the peace of knowing what God's will is for our lives. The Bible talks about letting go and taking one day at a time. God will help us to realize we cannot do it all, and we cannot be everything to others, either. Only He can do that. What does He say about boundaries in His Word?

Another helpful aid in living a balanced life is to have a mentor to remind you of God's truth and help you along the way. We all need at least one person to keep us accountable. If you do not have one, pray that God will bring someone with godly wisdom into your life to help you find and stay on the right path. None of us can do it alone, nor are we meant to. God did not call us to be completely independent and self-sufficient; we need to have a healthy balance.

Are you wearing yourself out by being overly busy or by trying to be completely independent? In Exodus, Jethro thought his son-in-law, Moses, was attempting to do too much. As the leader of the complaining Israelites, Moses was trying to judge all the disputes, whether minor or major. Finding personal time with God and handing down legal decisions for such a huge multitude was taking a toll on him. Jethro, in his wisdom, saw this and advised Moses to appoint others to take care of some of the easier cases (see Exodus 18 verse below).

Perhaps you are an exhausted mother of small children, a business executive with overwhelming responsibility, or a church volunteer experiencing burnout. Whatever season of life you find yourself in right now, take a lesson from what Moses had to do. Pray to discern if there may be tasks and opportunities you can delegate to another or just simply say no to when asked to do. Then trust God to meet those needs through someone else or in another way. Give yourself permission to defer and rest. Remember you are not the Statue of Liberty with a tablet that says, "Give me your tired, your poor, your huddled masses. . ." How burdened she looks! And she is not smiling, either. Listen—if we do not come apart from everyone and everything once in a while and take a break, we may just come apart! It offers one explanation for some of the anxiety in our nation today, doesn't it?

So, remember to not be too busy to seek God each day through prayer and reading His Word. Live each day, one day at a time and tomorrow will take care of itself. Concentrate on holding today in balance, and you will find that things will fall into place for the future. Let go and let God do His job because He is in control. Your responsibility is to be kind and help others when you can. The answers are found on our knees—pray, pray, pray! "God help me to remember that nothing is going to happen to me today that you and I can't handle together. Keep me in balance, Lord, so I can enjoy the life you've so graciously given to me." Be loved today, Iris

Tuesday
Scripture: "Very early in the morning, while it was still dark, Jesus got up, left the house and went off to a solitary place, where he prayed." (Mark 1:35)

Reflect, Activate: Even Jesus got away from all the people and busyness sometimes. Do you need to take some time today to do just that? Go to a place where you can be alone with Your Creator and converse with Him.

Wednesday
Scriptures: "But let your 'Yes' be 'Yes,' and your 'No,' 'No.' For whatever is more than these is from the evil one." (Matthew 5:37, NKJV)

"What does the Lord require of you but to do justly, to love mercy, and walk humbly with your God?" (Micah 6:8, NKJV)

Reflect, Activate: Of all the things you are committed to, is there any one of them (or more) that perhaps you need to step away from for a time? Pray to God for wisdom in how to let go of what you need to.

Thursday
Scripture: "Two people are better off than one, for they can help each other succeed. If one person falls, the other can reach out and help. But someone who falls alone is in real trouble." (Ecclesiastes 4:9-10, NLT)

Reflect, Activate: Think about when someone has been there to pick you up when you've fallen. It may have been through some encouraging words or an act of kindness or simply just sitting with you when you needed that. Is there someone you can do that for today?

Friday
Scripture: "You and these people who come to you will only wear yourselves out. The work is too heavy for you; you cannot handle it alone. Have them serve as judges for the people at all times, but have them bring every difficult case to you; the simple cases they can decide themselves. That will make your load lighter because they will share it with you." (Exodus 18:18, 22)

Reflect, Activate: How and who do you share "loads" with, in the past and in the present? Is there someone you can help in this way, or do you need to ask for help?

Saturday and Sunday
Scripture: "Be tenderhearted, be courteous...that you may inherit the blessing." (I Peter 3:9, NKJV)

Reflect, Activate: Look up the definition and synonyms of tenderhearted and courteous. Ask yourself (be honest)—"Am I those things? Do people know I'm a Christ follower by my actions?"

Prayer for Week: Lord, help me to focus on You first thing each morning. Guide me throughout my days to do the tasks You've called me to do but to be mindful of when I need to say "no" to the ones that are not meant for me to do.

WEEK 48

God's Faithfulness in the Deep Valleys

> "When you go through deep waters, I will be with you. When you go through rivers of difficulty, you will not drown. When you walk through the fire of oppression, you will not be burned up; the flames will not consume you." (Isaiah 43:2, NLT)

January 11, 2005, is a day my friend, Eleni, had her life changed forever. In an instant her husband and son were killed by a drunk driver. Larry was 44 and Jeremy was 20. They were on their way home from Walmart, where Larry had just picked Jeremy up from work.

My dear friend and her 18-year-old daughter, Larissa, suddenly found themselves encased in grief—a situation that neither ever imagined being in. The news was devastating for everyone who knew them. Why would God take two people who had touched so many lives and who were, by all opinions, going to continue sharing their faith to draw people to the saving grace of the Lord? Why would the God of love allow Eleni to now be without a husband and son and Larissa to be without a father and brother?

I can tell you that those questions are still present today. Answers have not suddenly surfaced with the passage of time. Are we wondering where Larry and Jeremy are? No. We are confident that they are with their Lord. They were both sold out for God and had been serving Him for a long time—Jeremy, his whole life. What remains, however, is the void they left behind.

Eleni shared with me a few years after it happened that she missed them even more than she did right after the accident.

I have observed her process of grief from afar mostly but up close and in person some, too. Through all the questioning and extreme pain, I have not seen Eleni's faith in God diminish. She never turned away from the Lord. Instead, she bared her heart as she prayed and cried out to Him. One of the first things she said to me when we went to the funeral was, "I know I should hate the man who hit them, but I don't." Amazingly, she still feels that way all these years later. Wow. That kind of grace can only come from God. Not hating that person has kept her from becoming bitter and has allowed her to move on in her life, even though it has not been easy.

Eleni and I have talked about what happened many times, and it seems like we always came back to these conclusions:

- We have to understand (and accept) that we are never going to understand the why.
- God has and will bring good out of it—somehow, although we many never see it this side of heaven.
- The man who hit them needs prayer that he will come to the Lord through this tragedy.
- God has never left Eleni. Without Him in her life, she surely would not have survived this.
- God is still on His throne. He is faithful and is still in control.
- He has protected Eleni in amazing ways during the years since the accident.
- Larry and Jeremy will always be missed, especially by Eleni and Larissa. The grief is that the rest of us are left behind.

The deep waters of grief have not overflowed Eleni, even though there were times when I know she thought she would surely drown. It has not been easy. But through it all, she is still standing and continuing to trust in God and that she will see her two loved ones again someday. That is the hope we have in Christ. Watching my dear friend trust her Lord while going through such a deep valley has helped me to grow in my faith.

So, be encouraged if any of you out there are grieving and missing a loved one right now. God loves you so much and is ready to help you through the pain and loneliness. Tell Him what you are feeling and that you need Him to hold you close to His heart. God's Blessing on you, Tammy

Tuesday
Scripture: "Blessed are those who mourn, for they will be comforted." (Matthew 5:4)

Reflect, Activate: When you have mourned the loss of a loved one, how have you been comforted? Write a list of verses that have or may help someone (or you) when mourning.

Wednesday
Scripture: "Therefore we do not lose heart. Though outwardly we are wasting away, yet inwardly we are being renewed day by day. For our light and momentary troubles are achieving for us an eternal glory that far outweighs them all. So we fix our eyes not on what is seen, but on what is unseen, since what is seen is temporary, but what is unseen is eternal." (2 Corinthians 4:16-18)

Reflect, Activate: Write down things that are temporary. Then write a list of the eternal, unseen things of God. How does looking at the eternal help you to have hope in the present?

Thursday
Scripture: "The LORD is close to the brokenhearted and saves those who are crushed in spirit." (Psalm 34:18)

Reflect, Activate: What does it mean to be crushed in spirit? What are some of God's promises (in addition to the above verse) for when we feel this way?

Friday
Scripture: "He heals the brokenhearted and binds up their wounds." (Psalm 147:19)

Reflect, Activate: How has the Lord "bound up" your wounds when you've been brokenhearted? Through reminding you of a promise in His Word? Maybe a friend has called to offer words of comfort at just the right time. Perhaps you felt His presence in a new and powerful way. If you know someone who is brokenhearted and needs comfort, be that for them today!

Saturday and Sunday
Scripture: "So do not fear, for I am with you; do not be dismayed, for I am your God. I will strengthen you and help you; I will uphold you with my righteous right hand." (Isaiah 41:10)

Reflect, Activate: Look up and then write down verses where we are told to not be afraid (there are many). The next time you are fearful, read over them to help God's peace to take over that fear.

Prayer for Week: Thank You, God, for always being with us—through even through the most intense pain and suffering. We know that you will never leave our side.

WEEK 49

Strive To Thrive

"...I have come that they may have life, and have it to the full."
(John 10:10)

You know the type. The woman had been in church all her life. She believed that every time the doors were open, one should be there. She had much of the Bible tucked away in her memory and could (and would) recite verses to you like nobody's business. She tried her best to be involved in every possible aspect of the church, every committee or function or ministry. Perhaps she did not outright broadcast about her many acts of ministry, but everyone knew. However, when people were around her, they felt a heaviness—a spirit of drudgery. She seemed to merely survive, void of any joy in the journey of living. This woman is a fictional character, but she could be real.

In fact, maybe all of us have been in her shoes at one time or another, or we know someone like her.

Jesus does not want us to get through this life with gritted teeth and white knuckles, hoping to hold on until the end, and dragging ourselves across the finish line when we finally receive the promise of heaven. He did not come only so we could go live with Him for all eternity in paradise. That is a most amazing future to look forward to, for sure, but there is SO much more. The verse above says He came so that we can live abundantly. He wants to give us a full and extraordinary life right now. Notice how it says, "This is eternal life." I take that as meaning it starts now—that we are able to know Him, even while still living on this earth in this mortal life.

God wants us to thrive in this life. To live with joy and purpose. Of course, there are seasons in our lives when we feel like all we are doing is surviving—those times of losing a loved one or great financial strain or other situations that can seem overwhelming. But the Lord understands our hearts when we are hurting and struggling. He wants to bring us through those things back to a place of blossoming, helping us to grow all along the way. Strive to thrive! Live in His joy, Tammy.

Tuesday
Scripture: "Now this is eternal life: that they know you, the only true God, and Jesus Christ, whom you have sent." (John 17:3)

Reflect, Activate: Read all of John, chapter 17, a beautiful prayer Jesus prays to God the Father. Write down the verses that particularly touch your heart.

Wednesday

Scripture: "But whatever is good and perfect comes to us from God, the Creator of all light, and he shines forever without change or shadow. And it was a happy day for him when he gave us our new lives through the truth of His Word, and we became, as it were, the first children in his new family." (James 1:17-18, NLT)

Reflect, Activate: How is your "new" life in Christ different from your old one when you didn't know Him?

Thursday

Scripture: "In his kindness God called you to share in his eternal glory by means of Christ Jesus. So after you have suffered a little while, he will restore, support, and strengthen you, and he will place you on a firm foundation." (1 Peter 5:10, NLT)

Reflect, Activate: Think back on a time when you were suffering in some way, whether physically or emotionally or spiritually. How did Jesus help you through it? Do you feel stronger now than before you went through the trial?

Friday

Scriptures: "Take delight in the Lord, and he will give you the desires of your heart." (Psalm 37:4)

"...being confident of this, that he who began a good work in you will carry it on to completion until the day of Christ Jesus." (Philippians 1:6)

Reflect, Activate: Think about one particular area in your life where you've watched the Lord help you progress towards something better. For example: jealousy, anxiety, an addiction, etc. Thank Him for the progress you've made and ask Him to continue to help you.

Saturday and Sunday
Scripture: "The blessing of the Lord makes one rich, and He adds no sorrow with it." Proverbs 10:22, NKJV)

Reflect, Activate: What does it mean that the Lord makes one rich? Do you think that means financially or otherwise?

Prayer for Week: Lord Jesus, help me to seek to thrive in this life and not just survive.

WEEK 50

Finding Joy and Contentment Amid Life's Chaos

"I remain confident of this: I will see the goodness of the LORD in the land of the living. Wait for the LORD; be strong and take heart and wait for the LORD." (Psalm 27:13-14)

Can we enjoy life—even when things are falling apart all around us? What does God say in the Bible about where our focus should be? He wants us to take pleasure in living, not concentrate on our trials and troubles. It is true that we are in this world and subject to its problems. So, what do we do when life takes over with failing health, financial losses, troubled relationships, etc.?

I was fortunate because I grew up in a very social family who promoted fun, but that did not make us immune to trials. Oh, no! When I was 8 years old, a debilitating illness left me with a lifetime of physical limitations and serious health issues. This put a strain on our family both economically and in our relationships. However, my parents acknowledged the pain and disappointments and were able to move on to provide recreation for all of us as best they could. I thank God for them, because they did prepare my siblings and me for life in so many ways. And they loved us at the same time.

In the same way, God teaches us how to find joy even in our struggles. He put us here on earth for fellowship with Him and so we would enjoy all He created for us. Unfortunately, Man, going back to the Garden of Eden, wanted to do his own thing.

(See Genesis, chapters 2 and 3.) From that moment on and due to humans desiring to go their own way, we now live in a fallen world. Sin and its consequences came to stay. Therefore, it is a given that we will experience the heartache and pain that goes along with living. But here comes the good news. We have hope through what Jesus did for us on the cross. We can savor this journey by not being under our circumstances but above them.

I really believe if we do it God's way and follow after Him, we will have less stress and more fun than we can imagine. Look at Deuteronomy 28 to see the instructions God gave the Israelites through Moses on this subject. In this chapter, the consequences of obedience versus disobedience of the commandments of the Lord are taught. Then in the New Testament, Jesus tells us where to place our energies (see Matthew 6:33 below). We might as well enjoy the ride—the journey—and allow God take care of the rest. He knows our needs and promises to meet them. Choosing joy while in a difficult circumstance is not easy, but necessary and certainly more fun. Try it!

With the right intentions, ask God to help you have integrity and that He would give you a fulfilling existence. Ask Him to help you with your thoughts and goals—that they would align with His will. Then watch as He guides you into an abundant life within His perfect plan for you. I can tell you from personal experience that you will enjoy your life greatly and with less stress than others who may not know Him. Living amongst all the chaos of this world is unavoidable, but we can choose to look to God to show us a life abundant in Him. In turn, we will have an impact on those around us as they watch us go through tough situations and still have contentment.

So, try joy and have some fun. Do the things you really delight in and have a passion for. Reach out to others when you can and watch His joy spread. God is here for our enjoyment, not to condemn us. Be blessed, my friends, and love and be loved. God is always right there with you! We are the ones who walk away sometimes, not Him. He is only a prayer away. He wants us to ask for His help to live a life full of peace and cheerfulness—will you call on Him today? Always moving forward in Christ, Iris

Tuesday
Scripture: "I have told you all this so that you may have peace in me. Here on earth you will have many trials and sorrows. But take heart, because I have overcome the world." (John 16:33, NLT)

Reflect, Activate: Think of someone who went through a time of great sorrow and then reflect on how the Lord brought them through it. How did seeing that boost your faith?

Wednesday
Scripture: "Consequently, just as one trespass resulted in condemnation for all people, so also one righteous act resulted in justification and life for all people." (Romans 5:18)

Reflect, Activate: Read Chapter 3 in Genesis and then read an account of the crucifixion and resurrection of Jesus in one of the four gospels in the New Testament: Matthew (chapters 27-28, Mark (chapters 15-16, Luke (chapters 23-24), or John (chapters 19-20).

Thursday
Scripture: "Seek the Kingdom of God above all else, and live righteously, and he will give you everything you need." (Matthew 6:33, NLT)

Reflect, Activate: What does it mean to you to "seek the Kingdom of God"? Maybe look up and write down Scripture that can help you in this quest.

Friday
Scripture: "You desire but do not have, so you kill. You covet but you cannot get what you want, so you quarrel and fight. You do not have because you do not ask God. ³ When you ask, you do not receive, because you ask with wrong motives, that you may spend what you get on your pleasures." (James 4:2-3)

Reflect, Activate: What is an example (either in your life or in others) when a person asked God for something but only for personal gain? Find examples in Scripture, too. How did those turn out for them?

Saturday and Sunday
Scripture: "The thief does not come except to steal, and to kill, and to destroy. I have come that they may have life, and that they may have it more abundantly." (John 10:10, NKJV)

Reflect, Activate: Write a list of all in your life which you feel you have an abundance of—maybe it's in finances or relationships. Thank the Lord for all He's provided for you!

Prayer for Week: Lord thank You that You give us a life full of joy even when we experience challenges and trials. Help me to spread that joy and love to others so that they may come to know You or know you better.

WEEK 51

Good News

"...but the angel reassured them. 'Don't be afraid!' he said. 'I bring you good news that will bring great joy to all people. The Savior—yes, the Messiah, the Lord—has been born today in Bethlehem, the city of David!'" (Luke 2:10-11, NLT)

Christmas is drawing near. There are lights to see, shopping to do, mountains of sweets to conquer. Then there are greetings to send and the office party to go to and cookies to bake—oh, my. It is the best time of the year, right? Not for everyone.

Growing up, I loved the feeling of the holiday and the excitement of it all. My parents always made sure that Christmas was special with the presents, decorations, and all the yummy goodies to eat. I loved the anticipation of wondering what was in the wrapped gifts under the tree. So, I was always dumbfounded when people said how they dreaded Christmas coming again—even hated it. How could anyone be downhearted during this holiday with so much fun tradition surrounding it?

I get it now. As an adult, I understand why this is not the best time of year for all people. Many struggle with handling all the good tidings they see others immersed in. They may not feel happy at all—in fact, they may be trying to just make it through while in a haze of depression. They do not want to deck the halls, and there is no joy in their world at the moment. All the twinkling lights may only magnify the darkness they feel. What about the wife facing the first Christmas without her husband? Or the man who has been looking for work for months and is struggling to provide for his family? Loss and troubles are a part of living throughout the year, but Christmas time can intensify emotions and deepen sorrows.

The Lord knows your heart. Whatever your story was before and whatever it is now—God's act of sending His Son, Jesus, to us as a baby trumps all. Because of His life here on this earth, we can live in victory no matter what we face. We can be assured if He loved us enough to leave all the glory of heaven to come to earth as a vulnerable baby, He surely will be by our side even when things get tough. We can agree with what the angels told the shepherds that night—it truly is good news.

So, remember those you know who are dealing with some difficulties this year. Reach out to them, if you can. Visit someone who is lonely or perhaps take a meal to a needy family. Let them know there is hope and that someone cares. Or if you are personally struggling this Christmas, take heart and try to focus on the ultimate gift that God gave over 2000 years ago. He loves you so much and wants to fill you with His peace and joy! In His Name, Tammy

Tuesday

Scripture: "Religion that God our Father accepts as pure and faultless is this: to look after orphans and widows in their distress and to keep oneself from being polluted by the world." (James 1:27)

Reflect, Activate: Can you visit a widow or orphan today or soon? Orphans can be adults, too – perhaps someone who has just lost a parent. Let them know they are loved and thought of.

Wednesday

Scripture: "The one who comes from above is above all; the one who is from the earth belongs to the earth, and speaks as one from the earth. The one who comes from heaven is above all." (John 3:31)

Reflect, Activate: Read verses 22 through 36 of John 3. John the Baptist was pointing people to Jesus in his ministry. Have you had someone (like a mentor) in your life who taught you about Jesus and their faith in a very humble way?

Thursday

Scripture: "The Word became flesh and made his dwelling among us. We have seen his glory, the glory of the one and only Son, who came from the Father, full of grace and truth." (John 1:14)

Reflect, Activate: Think about how Jesus left all the glory of heaven to live on this earth.

Friday
Scripture: "May the God of hope fill you with all joy and peace as you trust in him, so that you may overflow with hope by the power of the Holy Spirit." (Romans 15:13)

Reflect, Activate: Look up scriptures that talk about trusting God. How does putting our trust in Him cause peace and joy to come?

Saturday and Sunday
Scripture: "For God so loved the world that he gave his one and only Son, that whoever believes in him shall not perish but have eternal life." (John 3:16)

Reflect, Activate: How does looking forward to that eternal life give you hope for today and tomorrow for your time here on earth?

Prayer for Week: Thank You, Jesus, for leaving all the glory of heaven to come to this earth as a baby so that I can live forever with You in paradise someday.

WEEK 52

Christ Exclusive

"Jesus said to him, 'I am the way, the truth, and the life. No one comes to the Father except through Me.'" (John 14:6)

What makes Christ the exclusive truth? How do we know He is the "the way the truth, and the life"? Who do we listen to and gain godly insight from? My answer would be this: Any person or religion that puts man above God will lead you away from the truth. Conversely, when the Bible is taught and the name of Jesus is lifted up, truth will be established.

Growing up, I had good solid role models in my grandmother, mother, and several aunts who were all very family oriented. My parents were good to my siblings and me, and the Lord surrounded me with many Christian women. Even though I had a serious illness, my childhood was filled with fun and happiness. Television shows from the 50s were my entertainment because of the many physical limitations of my illness. June Cleaver (*Leave it to Beaver*), Harriet Nelson (*The Ozzie and Harriet Show*), and Donna Reed (*The Donna Reed Show*) were some of my favorites. Because of the example of these women, I found myself drawn to God and church and to being a housewife with a family. I remember thinking, "I want to be just like them!" I did not know it then, but these women were depicting values based on the Bible. In my early teens, I received the Lord as my Savior.

Together, all these role models taught me about bonding and being there for people when they are hurting. I learned that life has its challenges; it was never meant to be easy and fun all the time. But if we support each other and pray, things will work out with less worry and more trust. We do not necessarily get what we want all the time, but God always gives us what we need.

When I was 14, my whole world turned upside down when my parents divorced. The challenge of dealing with that broken relationship and my illness prompted me to look beyond the help this life had to offer. The peace and security the world brought was only momentary at best. Even at an early age, I felt empty—like something was missing.

I can also remember hearing my sister, who was much older than me, sharing stories about the rebellious 60s and 70s. The stable environment I longed for began to slip away, and this grieved my heart. The drug craze dominated the cultural of the youth, and the biblical principles I had come to know seemed to be a thing of the past. Young people were being drawn away from God and a healthy family environment. They wanted freedom from what they considered bondage. They searched for their own way, wanting no rules or strings attached. Material things and the ultimate high were the goals. The "I want to do it my way" philosophy spread like an epidemic. The resulting consequences, no matter the severity, were viewed as freedom and even happiness but only led to more bondage. Young people are naturally drawn to the excitement of being rebellious. However, they need the guidance from good solid role models so they do not fall into consequences they cannot come out of. To make matters worse, some Christians during this time were exhibiting more judgment than love. Many searching and wandering souls were cast off as difficult and in the way. What they really needed was to have someone demonstrate God's love to them.

Some people in a few churches I have attended have shown me that same kind of rejection because of my disabilities. They were human, and we all make mistakes, but fortunately I realized their actions were not an example of God's love. I was able to keep my faith because I came to understand that God would not treat me that way. It taught me to lean on Him alone. He sent many mentors so I could grow the way He intended for me to grow.

I would rather know that God has my circumstances in His hands and that everything will be all right, than to feel helpless to do anything with no one to turn to. Talk about feeling alone and hopeless! That is why we need a savior, and we have that in Jesus Christ. He is there to love and support us through the challenges and rejections in life.

So, how do we know Christ is the exclusive One—the only One? The next time you are in a tough situation, call on the name of the Lord. You will feel the peace and joy of His presence and a security that cannot be explained away.

I have experienced this, and you can, too. Read God's Word, the Bible, and see if He speaks something so profound and special to your heart that it changes your life. Yes, you still have to live in this world, but why not look to Him for the contentment that only He can bring? Your life will change; you will be joyous. He created you, and He wants you to be happy (see Deuteronomy 28). Investigate and see that God is who He says He is. With all my heart, I believe He is. I have been through many challenges in my life, and I have always found God's Word to be true. Blessings to you. Be loved today! Iris

Tuesday

Scripture: "So is my word that goes out from my mouth: It will not return to me empty, but will accomplish what I desire and achieve the purpose for which I sent it." (Isaiah 55:11)

Reflect, Activate: Search for other Scriptures that talk about the value of God's Word in the lives of believers.

Wednesday
Scripture: "And my God will meet all your needs according to the riches of his glory in Christ Jesus." (Philippians 4:19)

Reflect, Activate: Has there ever been a time when you had a desperate need and then saw God supply it in a unique or unexpected way, maybe even at the last minute? What need do you have today that you can go to Him in prayer and ask Him for? Keep the above verse in mind as you do so.

Thursday
Scripture: "Instead of your shame you will receive a double portion, and instead of disgrace you will rejoice in your inheritance. And so you will inherit a double portion in your land, and everlasting joy will be yours." (Isaiah 61:7)

Reflect, Activate: What blessing or gift do you have that you feel as if it is "over-the-top" and beyond what you ever could have hoped for?

Friday
Scripture: "In my distress I called to the LORD; I called out to my God. From his temple he heard my voice; my cry came to his ears." (2 Samuel 22:7)

Reflect, Activate: How has God heard you voice (prayer) today? How have you seen Him answer prayers for you and others around you?

Saturday and Sunday
Scripture: "You make known to me the path of life; you will fill me with joy in your presence, with eternal pleasures at your right hand." (Psalm 16:11)

Reflect, Activate: Search out other Scriptures dealing with the joy God gives us.

Prayer for Week: Lord, I know You are the way, the truth, and the life. I have seen it in my own life and in many other people's lives, too. Fill me with Your joy today, no matter what my circumstances look like.

A Final Word from the Authors

We hope this devotional has been a help and inspiration to you. Drop us a line on our website at: www.irisfsmith.com and share your thoughts with us. Thank you for allowing us to bring you on this journey of finding hope and encouragement through the study of God's Word and His promises. May the Lord bless you richly! Iris and Tammy

Please note: all pictures used within this book, except the cover, were taken by the author, Tammy Maseberg. Below is a partial list of picture locations:

Week 1, 13, 25: Rocky Mountains near Breckenridge, Colorado
Week 5: Grand Lake, Colorado
Week 7, 29, 33, 35, 45: Lakewood, Colorado
Week 9: Siena, Italy
Week 11, 17, 51: Evergreen, Colorado
Week 15: Heceta Beach near Florence, Oregon
Week 21, 47: Oregon Coast near Florence, Oregon
Week 27: Lookout Mountain, Golden, Colorado
Week 31: Jerusalem, Israel (House of Caiaphas)
Week 37: Sea of Galilee, Israel
Week 39, 43: Siuslaw River, Florence, Oregon

CPSIA information can be obtained
at www.ICGtesting.com
Printed in the USA
BVHW031453291121
622776BV00003B/59